Practice to Learn / Play to Win

The Answer To Your Best Golf

Mark Guadagnoli, Ph.D.

With contributions from Ryan Moore

Practice to Learn / Play to Win

© Mark Guadagnoli 2007

Book Cover Design & Typesetting by Martin Coote
martincoote@googlemail.com

Set in Frutiger light 11 on 14pt

First published in 2007 by;

Ecademy Press

6 Woodland Rise, Penryn,
Cornwall UK TR10 8QD
info@ecademy-press.com
www.ecademy-press.com

Printed and Bound by;
Lightning Source in the UK and USA

Printed on acid-free paper from managed forests. This book is printed on demand, so no copies will be remaindered or pulped.

ISBN 978-1-905823-15-4

Contents

SECTION I: Psychology of learning

SECTION II: Tools for learning

Section III: Finer points of learning

Acknowledgements

As you can imagine with most any book there are a great number of people who can share in the credit (or blame). A great big thank you to those who helped, including...

Scott Cowin (Head Golf Professional, Southern Highlands, Las Vegas), is a very good friend who used his expertise in an early review of the book. Not only did he improve the quality but he made suggestions for many of the practice sections.

Ryan Herrington (Senior Writer, *GolfWorld*) was kind enough to read through a very early, and I suspect painful, draft of the previous incarnation of this book. He made numerous good suggestions which boiled down to 'write what you know'. His help was invaluable to re-shape the concept of this book.

Steve Loy (Managing Partner/President & CEO, Gaylord Sports Management) who clearly went above and beyond to help promote the book. Even with the world spinning around Steve like a cyclone he found time to help a friend and it is not taken for granted.

Dwaine Knight (Hall of Fame Coach, UNLV Men's Golf) has taught me more about short game and golf in general than any other person. Many of the lessons this great man has taught me over the years are shown prominently in this book.

Mike Moore (Ryan's father and instructor) did a fantastic job reading and editing the book. He has a tremendous knowledge of the subject and this was quite clear in his review. Indeed, his contributions were so far reaching that they significantly impacted the finished product. At least as important for me, Mike is a valued friend who is supportive and inspirational on an ongoing basis. He is a role model to his family and to many of us beyond.

To say that **Ryan Moore** (PGA Tour Member) has been helpful does an injustice to his contributions. The many hours we spent through Ryan's college and early professional career talking about golf and life have clearly impacted the book. Our professional relationship became a tremendous amalgamation of the art and science of golf. The more we talked the more the lines blurred as to who served which role. No doubt, without Ryan this book would not have been what it is. This is why the book is written "with contributions from Ryan Moore," because Ryan is a significant part of what you will read. Finally, and more importantly to me, my time with Ryan has allowed a valued friendship to grow, and for that I am extremely grateful (see Prologue for details).

Prologue

In the acknowledgements I thanked Ryan Moore for his contribution to this book, but I think it is worth pointing out how years ago our conversations planted a seed that became the text you are about to read. Through Ryan's college and early professional career we spent many hours talking about golf and life. Early on this amounted to Ryan and I debriefing after a round, discussing what he did well what improvements needed to be made. Ryan mentioned several times that this helped him a great deal, but also during these conversations I found it fascinating to hear how he thought on the course and his philosophies about practice. I was also amazed at his ability to implement the suggestions made. Finally, working with Ryan and other members of the UNLV Men's golf team I found it interesting to see how 18-23 year old college students handled life's issues off the course. Lessons that turned out to be very helpful in understanding how life style can significantly affect your golf.

Eventually, Ryan, along with several other members of the golf team, took a course I taught called *Enhancing Mental and Motor Abilities.* Prior to this point most of our discussions had been about the science and art of golf with Ryan providing most of the art side of the equation and me the science. However, though discussions during and after the course our previously demarcated roles began to blur.

I have studied human performance and worked with collegiate and professional athletes for more than 20 years. I have published more than 100 articles and abstracts and presented this work to around the world including such countries as Canada, China, France, Germany, and Scotland, and have worked with athletes in sports including football, baseball, soccer, and track/cross country, and of course, golf. I have worked with PGA and LPGA instructors, PGA, LPGA, and Nationwide tour winners, many collegiate All-Americans, a US Amateur Publinks Champion, Masters and US Open participants, International JGA Tournament of Champions winner, Palmer Cup selection, Canadian National Team members, several AJGA and NCAA All-Americans, AJGA Polo Golf Junior Championship winner, Atlantic International Junior Championship winner, North Texas PGA Championship winner, a Junior World Champion winner, World Amateur winner, just to name a few. I am mentioning this because I want to add perspective that I have talked about learning and performance with a great many scholars and athletes and yet I have never dealt with an athlete who took ownership of the theories and knowledge of performance science the way Ryan did. To say that Ryan has been helpful in the conception of this book does an injustice to his contributions. Indeed, he has given me the great privilege of passage into the mind of a champion.

Introduction:
Practice to Learn | Play to Win

Have you ever wondered what is holding you back? Why don't you play the way you know you can play? The answer to these questions does not start with how you play, but how you practice. When you look at the way you play you are looking at the result not the cause. Although this may seem obvious most people don't realize that the way you practice has led to the way you play. If you have yet to find the answers in the books you read or the shows you watch, it is because often times these media overlook a major piece to the puzzle.

The world of golf improvement is largely populated by two types of books: those that deal with technique and those that deal with psychology. Books on technique speak about the mechanics of golf, including the swing, grip, stance, and other technical aspects of the game. The idea of these books is that if you can emulate what is suggested you will increase your ability. This is the first part of the golf success formula which states: *Your golf performance equals your ability minus interference.*

Psychology books approach the equation at a different level. They describe the proper mindset you should have for your best golf. In other words, they focus

PERFORMANCE EQUATION

Ability − Interference
= Your Best Golf

on interference. No doubt there is a certain romance in books on the psychology of golf. It would be great if just by thinking better on the course you could play better golf. Unfortunately, it doesn't quite work that way. Although your mindset is critically important to golf success (and success in life, for that matter), a good mindset with lousy skills won't do you much good. You need both a good mindset and a good skillset.

So here's the rub: Books on psychology and technique generally do a good job of telling you *what* to do, which is precisely what they are designed to do. What they are not designed to do is to tell you *how* to do it. For example, they tell you that to improve your golf you need to have a certain mindset but they don't tell you how to get that mindset. They don't tell you how to learn what they are professing. Don't get me wrong. I'm not knocking these books. They do what they are designed to do. The problem is that by itself, no one book completes the equation for success.

No one book completes the equation for success

Books on psychology and technique describe the two obvious parts of the performance equation, but there is a third part to the equation that is hidden from plain sight. Have you ever wondered why the books you've read didn't significantly lower your scores? The reason is simple. Psychology and technique books show you the picture of the treasure. They tell you what it looks like, but they don't give you a map showing you how to get there. The missing part of the equation is learning to learn; the missing part is the map to find the treasure.

Most golfers know what mindset they should have or what technique they should use, but they don't know the best way to make the mindset or technique into a habit. They don't know the best way to learn.

PRACTICE TO LEARN, PLAY TO WIN shows you the hidden part of the equation. *PRACTICE...* details proven real world methods for great golf. *PRACTICE...* provides specific keys to improving your ability, and presents a different way to think about practicing and playing, which in turn will substantially decrease your interference on the course. *PRACTICE...* gives you specific methods for improving your skillset and shows you how to translate this improved skill to the course.

PRACTICE TO LEARN, PLAY TO WIN is the map to less frustration and better scores

The three sections of the book are designed to build upon one another. They should be read in order. At the end of the book is a glossary of terms and several sample practice schedules.

The book is written to give you the tools and the mindset to learn, and the way to take your skills to the course. Along the journey, don't be surprised when your confidence rises as you use the book to organize your practice. Knowing what you're doing goes a long way in making your practice more efficient, which means less time practicing and more learning. More learning means increased ability, and there is nothing like increased ability to give your confidence a boost. So sit back and enjoy. I hope you have a very fun ride on your journey to great golf.

> **Section I** focuses on mindset or psychology, but not just the psychology of golf. It also focuses on the psychology of learning. Although little known, your mindset about learning goes a long way to dictate how much you will learn.
>
> **Section II** focuses on how to learn. Here you will learn how to learn two or three times faster than you learn now. You will also learn how to take your driving range success on to the course for great golf.
>
> **Section III** focuses on the framework that will supercharge learning and playing golf. Here we discuss goals, reasons for practice, and supercharging learning.

The journey to great golf begins here

section one: Psychology of Learning

Section I provides you with the mindset you need to have for efficient learning. As you will see, your mindset goes a long way to dictate how much you will learn.

The reward for learning greater patience, commitment and discipline is that you play golf with less frustration and more great shots. You must first understand the psychology of learning before you are given the tools for learning. If you are given a tool without understanding the basic way it should be used, the tool will do you little good. A wrench doesn't work as a screwdriver the same way a screwdriver doesn't work as a wrench. Understanding the purpose and idea behind the tools is what the psychology of learning is all about.

Welcome to Great Golf

The artist's blank canvas; the writer's first page; the golfer's first tee. Do they stifle action because of the limitless possibilities, or do they create excitement because of the opportunities ahead? Are these situations to be feared or relished? It is your choice. If you choose to embrace the opportunities you have, read on. If you choose to fear them, close the book. Not everyone is meant for greatness, but everyone has a choice.

Greatness is a matter of choice, not chance.

August 17, 2004 was a beautiful sunny day in Benton Harbor, a sleepy little town on the coast of Lake Michigan. Peter Tomasulo and Ryan Moore were engaged in a classic match-play duel at the prestigious 102nd Western Amateur Golf Championship. The event is said by many, including Tiger Woods, to be the toughest amateur golf tournament in the world. Tomasulo, a recent graduate of the University of California (Berkeley) was on a roll from his college team winning the NCAA Championship. He had played well all summer and this tournament was no exception. Moore, a senior-to-be at the University of Nevada, Las Vegas had won every tournament he had entered in the past three months, including winning the individual title at the NCAA Championship and his second US Amateur Public Links crown.

The match between the well acquainted competitors swayed back and forth all day at the Point O' Woods Golf Course. Tomasulo holed out a 7-iron from more than 160 yards to eagle the 16th hole. Moore answered by birdying the 17th to even the match.

Deadlocked going to the 18th tee Moore put his tee shot in perfect position in the middle of the fairway. The match's mojo seemed to be on his side. Tomasulo blocked his tee shot into the thick rough and had no choice but to chip out. Smartly, Moore hit his second shot to the center of the green about 12 feet from the hole. Just when it seemed all was lost for Tomasulo, he hit his third shot from about 130 yards and stuck it to within a foot of the hole to save par and extend the match.

On the first playoff hole neither player flinched, halving the hole with pars. Still handling the pressure of the moment, both players made their way to "the Point's" second hole, a 523 yard par-5 with a heavily protected green that course architect Robert Trent Jones guarded with a few well-placed trees and a creek in front.

Tomasulo and Moore both hit good tee shots. Tomasulo was a bit further out than Moore but had a great view of the green from his position in the center of the fairway. However, being 233 yards from a pin that was tucked on the right hand-side of the green was still no bargain. Tomasulo decided to go for the green in two. This shot would require all the skill and nerve Tomasulo could muster. To be successful required a shot that would carry the water hazard in front of the green, turn right toward the pin, and then land softly after its 233 yard journey. As difficult as it seemed, in truth there was no choice. He knew that this match would not be won by a par and he wasn't going to give this one to Moore. This match would have to be earned.

Tomasulo hit a 3-wood over the water. The ball held in the air and turned slightly toward the pin, but it didn't cut enough and ended up about 45 feet away from the hole. He hadn't done exactly what he wanted but he had forced Moore's hand. There was no lay-up option for Moore.

Moore was 217 yards from the pin but his position on the right side of the fairway meant that the huge oak tree between the water and green completely blocked his access to the hole. He stood on the right side of the fairway imagining several shots but none felt right. As his caddie, I stood in the fairway no more than 15 feet away, and yet he was in a world all his own. Moore was watching a scene from an imaginary movie playing in his head. The scene played over and over until it was right. Then it happened. He saw it perfect, he saw the shot, and he entered the zone. Everything slowed. There was no opponent. There was no crowd. There was only a player and his perfect vision of the shot. His laser focus drew the line he wanted the ball to travel and he mimicked the ball flight with his hand.

Moore pulled his weapon: a 4-iron. Behind the ball he made a few swings to show his body what his mind's eye had seen. He stepped into the shot and delivered a perfect swing of the club, sending a towering draw high over the right side of the oak tree. As the ball continued to turn it disappeared for a moment as it passed behind the tree's massive canopy. It seemed that seconds passed before the ball reappeared, dropping to the green eight feet from the pin. The hole, which Moore ultimately won, was over even before the putts were struck.. Ryan Moore had just thrown one more dagger into the heart of his opponent. This was just one more shot in a week of great play that included 41 birdies and 2 eagles in 151 holes of golf.

By no means was this Moore's first or last shot of great golf. *Golf World Magazine* called his accomplishments during that summer "the greatest amateur season in golf's modern era." His summer of superlatives included triumphs in the NCAA Championship, U.S. Public Links, Sahalee Players Championship, Western Amateur, U.S. Amateur, and the World Amateur. He followed this with a tie for 13th at the Masters, becoming only the third amateur in history to finish the Masters tournament under par, and later that year he became the first player since Tiger Woods to go from the college ranks to the PGA Tour without making a stop at a qualifying level. During each of these tournaments, there were points where Moore's focus and his belief of success were unsurpassed. There were moments, many of them, when Ryan Moore played to win.

As you read the story of Ryan at the Western you may be thinking that he was in the zone – that magical place where you are both the actor and the observer. That special time when everything is perfect. Your focus is crystal clear. Everything seems to move in slow motion, your swing feels effortless and the ball sails to its target as if you are watching it in a movie. It is true that Ryan, like many great players, has spent considerable time in the zone, but he didn't start there.

To understand the story of how Ryan and other great golfers get in the zone, you have to go back to the beginning. Great swings don't just happen, they are earned.

Great swings don't just happen, they are earned

For great golfers and golfers who want to be great, there is a logical path to travel to get where you want to be. The better you adhere to this path, the more efficient and less frustrating your travels will be. First, before you do anything else, decide that how you are playing now is not good enough. Decide that you want more. Decide that you will do what it takes to get more, and then let the rest of the book help you get there.

Decide that how you are playing now is not good enough. Decide that you want more.

The ZONE Alone Isn't Good Enough

> A great golf shot is a thing of beauty. Repeating it is an art. No great work of art was ever completed without effort. Michelangelo's 'David' was not created by a single strike of hammer on chisel. It was created through a process in which many hours were spent chipping away at granite. Golf is a similar work of art. Chip away with a proven process and you will succeed. Expect to find a great game with a single strike of the chisel and you will be disappointed. Many people look to the zone as that single strike but it is in fact only the polish applied to the masterpiece once its foundation is completed.

There is a certain amount of romance in books on the psychology of golf. The ideas that come from these books are nice and comforting. 'Thinking better on the course will make you play better golf.' 'Get in the zone for great golf.' No doubt these ideas ring true, but only if a host of other factors have been addressed first. The simple truth is that if you have lousy skills, the best thinking in the world will not make you a good golfer. To play your best golf means that you have to follow a simple formula:

Ability – Interference = Your Best Golf

Without ability, ridding yourself of interference does little good. Without ability, doubt will creep in and interference will increase. Without fulfilling all parts of the equation, all the thinking in the world will not make you a great player.

What is the zone, and why isn't it good enough?

One of my favorite movie lines about the zone comes from *The Last Samurai* with Tom Cruise. Cruise's character, a civil-war veteran, is in Japan on a mercenary mission. While on his mission, he is captured by a seemingly barbaric group of Japanese rebels. Rather than killing him, they allow him to live in their camp, and amazingly, they attempt to teach him to fight like a Samurai. Unfortunately for Cruise, he uses his western mindset to learn a skill derived from eastern philosophy. Like many achievers, he works extremely hard but he doesn't work smart. No matter how hard he works, he remains unable to fight with the speed and precision of the Samurai.

Along this journey Cruise meets a friend who is indeed a Samurai. The friend, noting Cruise's mounting frustration, says, "Free your mind so you can free your weapon." At this point in the movie time, slows and Cruise seems to channel through his weapon. His moves become instinctive, his speed lightning quick, and all of this happens by not thinking. This is the essence of the zone: Mindless perfect execution of well-honed skills.

Free your mind so you can free your weapon

Most people think of the zone as a magical event that just happens, and if you've been there, you have probably felt that it was effortless as well. What you are feeling is the culmination of skills that have been practiced and are now free to flow. In fact, the zone requires that the conscious mind has committed skill to memory, and then the unconscious mind is able to unleash the skill free of interference. This means that being successful in the zone requires two steps. Step 1: Create the skill necessary for success. Step 2: Get out of your own way and let the skill happen. If you fail to develop the basic skills, getting out of your own way won't help you much.

> **The Zone Requires Two Steps**
>
> **Step 1:** Create the skill necessary for success.
>
> **Step 2:** Get out of your own way and let the skill happen.

Sam Snead and Byron Nelson are great examples of this two-part method. Snead was an intuitive genius who knew that playing for the intrinsic joy of the game would create a zone-type feeling, but he also had the discipline to develop his skills. Byron Nelson once said that in his epic 1945 season he would play rounds so focused on hitting good shots that he never knew how he had scored until after the round. Even though one of Nelson's greatest attributes was his mental approach to the game, he only briefly mentioned the importance of it in his instruction books. About all he ever said in this regard was, "Every great player has learned the two Cs: how to concentrate and how to maintain composure." When Nelson was asked why he talked so little about such an important aspect to his success he replied, "Aw, people didn't talk about that sort of thing in those days."

> If you would allow me to digress for a moment I would like to say a few words about Byron Nelson. Most people know of Mr. Nelson's golf highlights which include winning 11 tournaments in a row, during which time he had a 68.33 stroke average. Amazingly, during this same time he finished in the Top 10 in 65 consecutive tournaments. The golf accolades can go on for some time, but at least as important was Mr. Nelson's contribution off the course. Mr. Nelson was known as the consummate gentleman and was eager to help others. Perhaps Ken Venturi summarized Mr. Nelson best when he said: "You can always argue who was the greatest player, but Byron is the finest gentleman the game has ever known."

Fast-forward half a century and we now see the importance of the mental side of the game. In a recent article in *Golf Magazine*, it was suggested that "as the ball-striking abilities of the game's best have be-come more uniform, there is a growing acknowledgment that what most separates the top-level players from others is their mental ability." Tiger Woods acknowledged this by saying, "My greatest gift is my creative mind."

We all admire that golfer who stares down a 6-foot putt and drains it to win a tournament or the player who can pipe a 300 yard drive down the center of the fairway when the pressure is on. I'm included in this. In fact, I'll volunteer to drive the bandwagon that shouts about the importance of mental skills for peak performance. However, there is an incredibly important point that is missed in all this. Not everyone has great ball striking abilities! Remember, to be in the zone requires two parts to the equation. Without skill the first part of the equation is not satisfied. First you must develop the skill **then** free your mind. Develop a solid foundation before you build your house on it or under times of stress the house will crumble to the ground.

Develop a solid foundation before you build your house on it or under times of stress the house will crumble to the ground

When you try to free your mind with underdeveloped skills, it creates two types of problems. First, freeing your mind is easier said than done. This is especially true when you don't have a lot of confidence. Very few things will develop confidence in your game better than improving your skill. Second, freeing your mind doesn't create great skill, it only allows you to get out of the way of the skill you have. The Samurai doesn't free his mind *before* he studies his craft. He spends thousands of hours learning swordsmanship, balance, and strategies. Only then does he free his mind to surrender to what he has learned. Byron Nelson, Sam Snead, Tiger Woods and others have been able to use their excellent minds in conjunction with their excellent mechanics, not in the absence of mechanics. You need to have appropriate skill before you free your mind. Like in the story with the Samurai, working hard is not good enough. You need to work smart if you want to get where you want to be. The key to working smart is to commit to a system that creates efficient practice, much more fun on the course, and better scores. The next chapters explain the system that does exactly that. To take full advantage of this system you must commit yourself to it.

Freeing your mind with poor skills will let you play the best poor performance you can play. Is that good enough for you?

> ### Key Points
>
> ♦ First develop the skill, then freeing your mind will allow great things
>
> ♦ Refined skill is the foundation from which good things happen in golf
>
> ♦ A good mind with bad skills only lets you play less bad golf

All Practice is Not Equal

> "Nobody – but nobody – has ever become really proficient at golf without practice, without doing a lot of thinking and then hitting a lot of shots. It isn't so much a lack of talent; it's a lack of being able to repeat good shots consistently that frustrates most players. And the only answer to that is practice."
>
> *Jack Nicklaus*

There is a fundamental question that is often overlooked: What's so important about practice? Let's say that you have the perfect mindset for golf. You never get rattled, you are always positive on the course, and you are excellent at staying in the moment. Congratulations. This means that you will be able to optimize the skills you have. Here's the problem: Optimizing bad skills only allows you to have less bad results. In other words, if your mindset is great but your golf skills leave something to be desired, you will only be a little better than someone who does not have good mindset. Because a good mindset can't overcome bad skills.

A good mindset can't overcome bad skills

Perhaps more to the point, it is very rare for a competitive individual to have a great mindset without first having good skills.

For all golfers in the US with a registered handicap, the average handicap is about 16 (calculated as roughly 80% of raw score). This means that they average a little worse than bogey golf. You may be thinking, "Bogey golf. That's not too bad." Remember, we're talking about the average golfer with a handicap, but not all golfers register a handicap. For those golfers without a handicap, the average is much higher. So for the real average golfer, or for that matter, even the golfer that is a little better than average, it is difficult to have a great mindset if you aren't sure where your ball is going to go. Also if you are like most golfers, you know that if your skills improve so does your confidence and a good mindset is much easier with good confidence.

> The problem of a poor attitude doesn't always resolve itself when your skills improve. Most people hold themselves to a higher standard as they improve. If this is you, the same shot that wouldn't bother you as a lesser player now really gets under your skin. To deal with this, work on your mental skills and physical skills in concert with one another. Doing this will allow you to improve your skills and create the mindset you need for those new and improved skills.

For most people, confidence and skill go hand in hand. The better your skill, the more confident you are. The more confident you are, the easier it is to get out of your way and let your skill take over. Improving skill is key, and as Mr. Nicklaus said, focused practice is the only answer to improving skill. He said that to learn you need to do "a lot of thinking and then hitting a lot of shots." As is common with great players, no scientific basis was required for Mr. Nicklaus to hit the nail on the head. Hitting balls alone doesn't do the job, thinking is a critical part of the equation.

Herein lies the problem. Let's say you've tried to practice and you just don't get better. If this is the case, you may be frustrated and left with the question, why practice? I mean, why keep banging your head against the wall? The real question is, why practice wrong when you could practice right? It isn't about *how much* you practice. It is about *how* you practice.

Hard work does not equal smart work, and smart work is what gets the job done

Practice correctly and you will learn. Practice incorrectly and you will get frustrated, and this will lead to higher scores. So if you practice now but you don't get better, it is not that you are incapable of improving, it is more likely that you are going about it wrong. If you want to change the outcome you must change the process.

To learn effectively, you have to practice effectively, and most people simply do not know how to practice effectively. This isn't meant as a slap in the face of golfers. Most golfers try to do

> "The definition of insanity is doing the same thing and expecting a different outcome."
> **A. Einstein**

their best based on what they know – it's just that a little better training would go a long way. Think of it this way: If you want to become a surgeon, you don't just pick up a scalpel and give it a try. You go through training to learn the basic techniques, and you don't work on your own until you have a good idea of what you're doing. This is not the way most people treat golf.

Sometime for the fun of it, go to your local driving range and before you hit balls, just watch for a few minutes. My guess is that you will see that the majority of people hitting a lot of balls without any apparent improvement. This may be your habit as well. If it is, your golf life is about to change. By knowing the art and science behind proper practice, you can separate yourself from the pack. The bottom line is that all practice is not equal, and the more you know how to practice the more you will see improvement on the range and on the course. Because all practice is not equal, the better you understand the do's and don'ts of effective practice, the faster you will see better scores on the course.

All practice is not equal

The exceptional golf you see on television doesn't just happen, it is earned. No matter how much natural talent you may have, you will never reach **your** potential unless you learn how to practice effectively. Not reaching your potential may sound like bad news. In fact, if you consider that you've gotten where you are without the benefit of the secrets we're going to talk about, this is actually good news. It's like you've been training for a marathon with a 50 pound pack on your back and you are about to learn how to take it off.

In the chapters to follow, you will learn how to play your best golf because you will learn how to get the best from each practice session.

The methods explained here have been used to speed up learning dramatically. In fact, it has been scientifically established in my research and that of my colleagues that appropriate practice can speed learning four or five times the normal rate.

Efficient practice can speed learning four or five times the normal rate

This means that you hit a lot fewer balls on the range but you play a lot better on the course. This may sound too good to be true, but it's not; it's a fact. I'm not talking about a magic pill or hypnotism or some far-out method. I'm talking about letting science work for you. It takes a little patience and discipline, but this is a good thing. We can all use a little more patience and discipline. So if you are truly committed to reaching your golf potential, read on. The road map to a journey of much greater skill and more enjoyable golf is right in front of you.

> I worked with a tour player who had pain shooting through his wrist every time he even slightly mis-hit a ball. As you can imagine, this was a major problem. In looking at video, we realized that his swing had changed, which was either because of the problem or had helped to create the problem. Regardless, he needed to make some major changes in his grip and swing before the season started. The problem was the season was to start in three weeks. These kinds of changes take a year or more for most golfers. By using efficient practice techniques, he was making cuts with a new grip and swing in four weeks, and by the end of the season he had earned nearly a million dollars. The methods work if you do.

PRACTICE VERSUS LEARNING

I have a secret to tell you. The secret is that I know how you can learn faster – much faster – and with less frustration. What would you think if I told you that I know a way to speed up your learning so that you can learn at least twice as fast as your current rate? And what if I told you that this "trick" will actually take less time and you will learn more? In golf, this means less time on the practice range and better scores on the course. Understanding and using good practice techniques will give you a tremendous advantage over those who don't know the secrets.

The first part of the secret is to think differently about what happens during practice. Practice performance does not tell the whole story, but most people have in mind that they practice as they play, and yet these same people have seen that this isn't the case at all. For example, have you ever had a good practice but you went out the next day and didn't play well? If you are like most people, it has happened more than once.

When you practice but don't get any better, it is generally the result of poor practice technique. At best, using poor technique is a waste of time. At worst, it can actually hurt your game. The good news is that correct practice is as positive as incorrect practice is negative. In fact, one of the reasons golf lessons are so helpful is that they often simulate many of the correct ways to practice.

A TALE OF TWO PLAYERS

Player 1 was a very good junior golfer and became a good college golfer. The problem was that from his freshman year in college through his junior year, he got worse. Because of this he became quite frustrated and decided to try something new. That is when we started working together.

One day he confided in me that he was practicing as much as four hours a day and couldn't get any better. As you can imagine, he was becoming very frustrated. He was increasing the amount of practice and his scores were going up!

The first thing I did was watch one of his practice sessions. He went to the putting green to start practice, and I stayed back to watch. I was prepared to watch for four hours to understand what was going on. It only took about 45 minutes to get a very clear picture.

First, I noticed that in 45 minutes at the practice area he actually engaged in practice a total of 12 minutes. The rest of the time he spent talking with people on the putting green, hitting putts without paying attention, and hitting 'hit-and-drag' putts. Hit-and-drag putts are those putts that immediately after you hit them, you realize they're going to miss. So even before they stop rolling, you reach out with your putter and drag the ball back.

For 45 minutes Player 1 would talk, hit a putt, talk a little more, "practice" 45-60 foot putts without really paying attention to them, and hit a lot of hit-and-drag putts. He was not engaged in the process, and he was not practicing the skills he needed for better golf. In other words, what he focused on and how he was going about it was not helping to make him a better golfer. This is a bad combination. At this pace, I could see that his four-hour practice was actually less than one hour of poor practice. However, in his mind he practiced four hours each day and didn't shoot better scores. This, as I mentioned, led to frustration, which in turn led to worse scores.

The first thing that I taught Player 1 was how to avoid talking to people while practicing. I'm not suggesting that all talking during practice is bad. I'm suggesting that spending the majority of your time being unengaged in the process makes for inefficient practice. Player 1 was a very friendly person and people routinely talked to him on the putting green. Just ignoring them would have been rude, and so it was best to put up a do not disturb sign in the way of headphones. The funny thing was that the headphones were not playing music, but they kept people away. When he had a scheduled break, he simply took the headphones out of his ears, had a short conversation and then returned to his work with the headphones on.

The next thing we did was plan out three 30-minute practice blocks in which he practiced one skill area for 30 minutes. For example, he started with 10 minutes of distance drills followed by 10 minutes of 3-4 foot putts from around the hole, 5 minutes of pace putts, and finally 5 minutes of 6-12 foot putts. Wedge play included bunkers, bump and run, and chips, each for about 10 minutes. Full swing was 7-10 minutes each of wedges, mid-irons and woods, with the last 5 minutes being alternating clubs. (Some of these methods/schedules are listed in the appendix of this book).

By the end of one hour of practice, he was mentally exhausted because for the first time in his life he had been engaged in practice for 60 minutes. The good news was that that he had learned much more than he did in any of his normal four-hour practice sessions. The point was not just to shorten practice to 60 minutes; after all, for most high level players, that just isn't enough time. The point is that the quality of practice is far more important than the amount of time you spend at the practice facility.

> "It isn't the hours you put in at practice that count. It's the way you spend those minutes."
>
> **Tony Lema**

The player improved dramatically over the next few months; so much so that he went on to play some PGA tour events. Unfortunately, this story is not a fairy tale. The player's 'girlfriend' decided she didn't want him traveling so much and the only way to keep the relationship alive was to quit golf. What can I say? Relationships are much less predictable than practice methods.

Player 2 was also a good junior player and was playing golf at one of the top college programs in the country. Although he had improved over his first two years, during his third year he hit a common road block. Not only was he not getting better, his scores were getting worse. It is not uncommon for players to reach a point where they continue to practice but they don't get better. When this happens, the natural tendency is frustration, and this is exactly what happened to Player 2. In fact, it had gotten so bad he was no longer one of the top five players on the team and because of that, he wasn't on the traveling squad for tournaments.

One day early in the spring season, Player 2 came in to talk about what was going on. He was a hard worker, so I suspected that problem was not the quantity of his practice. As we talked about how he practiced, it became clear that the culprit was the way he was practicing. He used the common method of "banging balls" on the range for most of his practice, and when he did play it was the same course from the same tee shots every time. We revised his methods of practice, much like I will show you in the rest of the book, including the last section that actually provides sample practice schedules.

Player 2 started making dramatic improvements. Not only was he hitting the ball better, but he was becoming more battle-ready. About three months after the first session with his new practice method, he won one of the top collegiate tournaments of the season, beating the number 1 rated collegiate player in the country.

Practice can be a powerful ally or a frustrating foe.
You choose.

EXAMPLE SCHEDULE FOR EVERYDAY GOLFERS

If you're like most people, you don't have the time or inclination to practice four hours a day. Commonly, most golfers report that they would like to only practice enough to maintain or improve their game a little. I'm not one of those people. I have a sneaking suspicion you aren't either, or you wouldn't have gotten this far in the book. You probably would love to get better at golf. You may even like to practice, but if you have a job, family, or other responsibilities that keep you from practicing hours each day, how do you get better?

If you have a job, family, or other responsibilities that keep you from practicing hours each day, how do you get better?

In the next section we will talk about some specific practice principles and proven methods of efficient practice. Once you understand these principles you will be able to have smart practice and this will lead to more learning and better golf, but you still may have a time issue on some days. The short section below is written so you have no excuses. If you have 15 minutes in your day that you can free up, you can practice golf.

WHAT IF YOU ONLY HAVE 15 MINUTES?

Not long ago I was at a charity function for the American Cancer Society. It was a wonderful affair with support from Lance Armstrong and a private concert from Sheryl Crow. I was seated at a table with a couple of friends and about eight people I did not know. Through casual conversation we got to the "What do you do?" question. I said that I'm a performance enhancement specialist. Since I live in Las Vegas the phrase 'performance enhancement' raised a few eyebrows as you can imagine. I went on to explain that I work with athletes to help them improve their athletic performance (I also decided to change my job description). Within a matter of seconds the men at the table focused the conversation on golf and a common problem among most good players.

"I just don't seem to have any time to practice and it is very frustrating. Is there anything that I can do about it?"

The question is not unique. I hear it quite a bit. I generally follow with a question myself.

"Do you have 15 minutes in a day to practice?"

"Sure, but I can't even get to the course in 15 minutes."

"Then don't go to the course to practice," I respond, usually creating an uncomfortable silence of a few seconds.

If you only have 15 minutes, the way to get the most out of practice is to not use your time to drive to a practice facility. For the large majority of people who don't live on a golf course, the drive to practice is more than 15 minutes. However, that doesn't mean you can't get in quality work. In fact, 15 minutes a day could make a huge difference in your golf game if you do it correctly. Practicing grip, stance, and posture in front of a mirror will ensure that you have a solid foundation of the fundamentals. Likewise, practicing drills such as half swings, take away, etc. for 15 minutes each day will make that part of your swing more automatic, and automatic is what will take over when you play.

So if you think about it that way, having 15 minutes is not a limitation, it is an opportunity. Time is only a limitation if you let it be. If you have limited time and/or resources, then you will need to use more creativity, but you can still get the job done. As you will see later, attitude and a plan can resolve a lot of issues.

> ### *Key Points*
>
> ◆ Get the right mindset for practice. The right mindset can go a long way.
>
> ◆ Smart practice is much more important than hard practice
>
> ◆ A little bit (15 minutes) can add up over a long time, just do a little each day.

Good to Great

> *The River Creatures*
>
> Huddled close together were tiny river creatures clinging to a moss covered rock. As the water rushed over them they shivered from the cold and complained that they were miserable. Their entire life was holding on to this rock. Finally one of the creatures announced that he was going to let go of the rock and let the river take him wherever it chose to take him.
>
> *"You can't just let go"* one of the creatures countered. *"You don't know where you will end up."*
>
> *"It doesn't matter where I will end up"* the brave creature said. *"I know that I don't like where I am and so I am willing to take the chance."*
>
> And with that the creature let the river take him to his destiny.

I'm not sure where I first heard the story of the river creature and frankly I had forgotten about it until a few years ago when I read an excellent book entitled *Good to Great.* It is about the art of business but when I read the story I couldn't help but see how it could easily be turned into a story of golf. *Good to Great* describes how several major companies went from being *good* companies to *great* companies, and they did this based on a relatively simple shift in their approach. Like the river creature, the companies decided that being good was not good enough, and they decided to let go and do something great.

This may sound simple enough but in real life people rarely take action to become great. They may decide that good is not good enough but that doesn't mean they will do something about it. Why? Sometimes it is fear. Sometimes people have the best of intentions but they just don't know how to go about making the change. Part of the purpose of this is to tell you how to let go of fear and make the necessary changes to go from good to great.

If you are one of the few who choose greatness you will be in good company. Those people like you who choose the road less traveled often become the icons of success. In the golf world we often think of golfers like David Toms, Jim Furyk, and Chad Campbell as being very successful, but they didn't just wake up one day as great golfers; they worked their way there. Chad Campbell worked his way up through mini-tours, Q-school, the Nationwide tour, and is now a multiple winner on the PGA tour. And don't count him out for a major in the next few years. Just like Campbell, Toms and Furyk spent many years to become "overnight successes". Perhaps the most classic example is that of Vijay Singh. In 2004 Vijay hit the $10 million dollar mark in a season. It was the first time in history that was done. As a golfer struggling to get through European Q-School, Vijay worked as a bouncer in a Scottish nightclub. He also worked as a teaching pro in Borneo giving $10 lessons. That's right; the $10 million dollar man once gave $10 lessons; So much for an overnight success. These people all had in mind that being a good golfer wasn't good enough. They were willing to do what it took to be great. They had the talent, work ethic, and belief structure to make it happen.

The opening story in this book talked about Ryan Moore. He is yet another example of good to great. I've been to a lot of golf courses with Ryan and I have heard many people comment that Ryan just walked on to the PGA tour and got his card. Although he did become one of only five players in the history of the PGA to get his card from playing on exemptions, to understand the true story you have to go back a few years. There was a lot of work and soul searching that came before the success.

During his sophomore year in college at UNLV, Ryan was a good collegiate golfer, but he wasn't great. At least he wasn't playing like a great golfer. During a qualifying round for a college tournament, Ryan came off the 12ᵗʰ green at his home course. He was disgusted about missing a putt and he was muttering to himself and kicking his putter. I stood next to Ryan's college coach, Dwaine Knight, and watched the scene unfold. Coach Knight is a Hall of Fame coach and he has seen plenty of talented collegians. In previous years at UNLV he coached Adam Scott, Chad Campbell, and Chris Riley. Coach Knight turned to me and said, "If he ever learns to embrace the challenge, he will be something special." Within six months Ryan had learned to embrace challenge like nobody I had ever seen before. It was a simple shift in attitude and practice that took Ryan from good to great but it all started with him making the decision that good wasn't good enough. The next year he won every major college and amateur award there was including the Nicklaus Award for the top college golfer and the Hogan Award for the country's top amateur.

"If you want to improve you have to be willing to let go of where you are" – *Ryan Moore*

Finally, the last example I have for good to great is actually an example of extremely good to great, and that is Tiger Woods. I have to admit that I wasn't a great fan of Tiger when he first came out on tour. I thought he was a little smug and aloof. I now admit that I was mistaken – it was his extreme focus that I was observing. Several times I have seen Tiger work out with his trainer Keith Kleven and I can honestly say that I have never seen someone work harder or smarter than Tiger. More to the point, twice in a relatively short career so far Tiger has decided that very good is not good enough. Twice he has changed a swing that propelled him to #1 in the world, and both times he became even greater as a result of it. Not many people are willing to let go of great to get greater.

NOT EVERY STORY TURNS OUT LIKE A FAIRY TALE

What about all those who never got any better? What happened to the person who wanted to get better so they took lessons and got worse? And let us not forget those unfortunate souls who seemed to crumble ever so painfully in the public eye. To go from good to great you have to completely let go of good. That is very difficult to do, especially if you had success at good. Change takes a commitment of body and mind. Bailing out in the middle of a journey lands you stranded on the side of the road and going nowhere fast.

What do Tiger Woods, Ryan Moore, Vijay Singh, David Toms, Jim Furyk, and Chad Campbell have in common? They all have incredible talent, they all have great patience and confidence, and they all decided that good was not good enough.

GOOD TO GREAT

In the book *Good to Great* there is a graph that shows the stock value of

Recently I was at Harvard University as a Visiting Scholar. While there I presented a learning theory known as Challenge Point Theory, the same idea presented in the second section of this book. One of my friends at Harvard is Dr. Dan Schacter, a noted memory expert and an excellent golfer. After the presentation he pointed out that based on the Challenge Point theory of learning, Tiger needed to change his swing to maintain his level of challenge and dominance of the game. I believe Dan is exactly right and we will talk about this more in the next section.

several companies over a 30-year period. The graph in the book is similar to the one shown below. It is also similar to one we'll talk about later that shows how people go from good to great with golf.

One of the things you may notice about the graph is that for a while all the companies plodded along at a similar pace, and then about half way along something began to change for some of the companies.

Graph reading 101: As a college professor I take time at the beginning of each semester teaching students how to read graphs. It seems to be a lost art among old scientists, so perhaps it is worth a short reminder here. The vertical (y) axis generally shows performance. The higher up you go the better the performance. In the case of good to great, the performance is stock value. The higher up the y-axis the higher the stock is performing. The horizontal (x) axis shows scale. In this case it is time in years. The further to the right you go the more time passes. So if the graph line goes up as it moves to the right, it means that the stock value increases over time. This may be pretty obvious to you with the current graph but it is good to learn now because future graphs will be a bit more complicated.

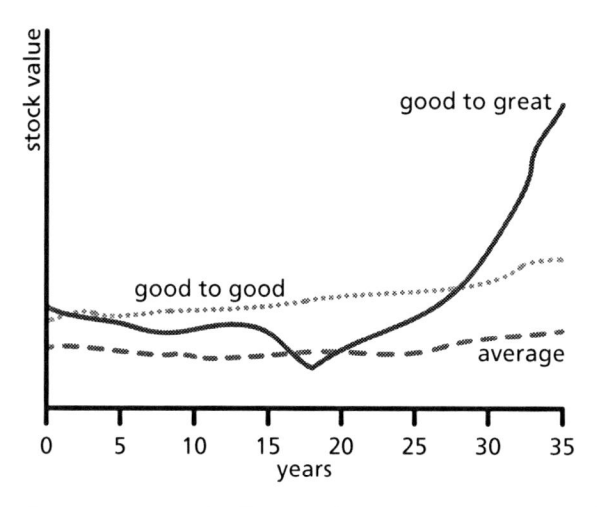

Good to great graph. Shows what happens to companies
over the years as the do or do not change philosophies.

The dashed line represents the average companies. Over time they get a little better, but all they are really doing is keeping pace with the other average companies. This is like the guy who plays golf every once in a while at company functions or outings with friends. During every round he can expect a few good shots and a several not so good shots, and his scores stay pretty much the same from year to year.

The dotted line represents companies that start out good and stay good over the period. These are called good-to-good companies. The golf equivalent to this is the golfer who starts out pretty good but never seems to get a whole lot better. He rarely shoots high numbers but never goes really low.

The solid line companies are the companies that decided good was not good enough. They wanted to be great and they were willing to sacrifice the certainty of good for the possibility of great. These companies are known as good-to-great companies. The management of the good-great companies made two critical decisions that set their new course into action. They decided that good was not good enough for them, and they decided that they would risk the certainty of good for the possibility of being great. It is also important to note that for the large majority of these companies the changes came from within, which is a nice a parallel between the companies and your golf game. For you to go from good to great the same needs to happen. Utilize coaches and trainers to help but if the change doesn't start from within and isn't fueled by you all the support in the world won't make a difference. The golfer who wants to improve has to be willing to give up the habits that are keeping him from being great. Habits of good need to be replaced by habits of great.

Habits of good must be replaced by habits of great

In the story of the companies none of the changes happened over night. It took years to change, and during those years the companies struggled at times. For golfers, it may not take years to change but it will take time and effort. Swing changes, mindset changes, and other changes of habits take time. There was no magic potion that made the companies good one day and great the next, and there are no magic potions for you to go from good to great. However, there are certain things you can do that will ensure you will get where you want to be.

You may have noticed that the good-to-great companies took a step back before they became great. In fact, many people, just like companies, may actually get a little worse before they become great. This is not so surprising. Any time you make a change you are disrupting the system that is in place. This may cause you to struggle for a bit while you are learning the new system. Remember what I mentioned before about Tiger reworking his swing? People thought he was crazy. He was already the best golfer in the world but that wasn't good enough for him. He 'struggled' for a while, but eventually he became an even more dominant player. Think also of Lance Armstrong. He was a good cyclist before cancer but he wasn't great. His cancer left him physically and mentally devastated and as a result his performance curve took a huge dip. But Lance showed one of the most remarkable "can do" attitudes ever seen in sport. The cancer reshaped his body, but because of his attitude the cancer also gave Lance the motivation to reshape his mind, and in doing so he became the world's greatest cyclist.

Armstrong won his first Tour de France *after* cancer, not *before*

One of the things Lance and Tiger have in common is that although they may have gotten frustrated, they never gave up working toward greatness. They never gave in and they never gave up.

GOOD (TO BAD) TO GREAT

The good to great story happens in golf just like it does in business. A few years ago a colleague and I ran a golf experiment. Little did I know at the time that we were about to stumble across the idea of good to great, with a slight deviation along the way. In the experiment we were trying to understand the effects of video feedback on learning the golf swing. At the time, video capture systems were just coming on to the market and I wanted to know if they were worth the expense. In other words, did they really help? To test this idea we recruited 60 golfers from around Las Vegas and divided them into three groups. Each group practiced for 90 minutes a day for four days. One group got no instruction during their practice. They just hit balls at their own pace for 90 minutes. The logic behind this group is that we wanted to see if people would improve by just practicing. Most people would tell you that they would be better if they only had time to practice but they just don't have the time. We wanted to see if this was true.

A second group got golf instructions during their 90-minute session. These instructions were regular golf lessons given by a PGA professional. The third group got video instructions during their 90-minute session. These instructions were like regular golf lessons but rather than just telling the golfer what they were doing the golfer was also shown a video of their swing. All golfers were tested the day before the first lesson (pretest) and two days after the lessons finished (post-test). Both the pretest and the post-test were designed as a skills test and were meant to simulate an on-course situation.

From the pretest we found out that there was no difference between groups. We did this so that if there was a difference after lessons we would know it was because of the lessons, rather than the groups being different to start.

Can you guess which group did best on the post-test? If you guessed the video group you guessed wrong. They were actually the worst. The group that got no instructions did best! That's right, no instruction was better than instruction, and getting video instruction actually hurt performance.

If we ended here I am sure that I would have a lot of teaching pros angry with me because basically the results of the study suggest it is a waste of time and money to get lessons, especially video lessons. In fact, the PGA professional working on the study and all those I tell the story to cringe at this point in the story. Fortunately, we did not stop with the post-test right after the lessons. In fact, the next part of the study cleared up the picture dramatically. We asked all the golfers to keep practicing for two weeks and then we called them back for a second post-test. The results changed dramatically as you can see in the following figure.

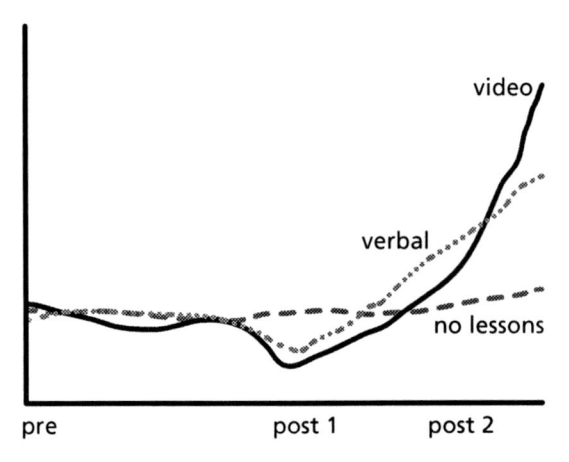

Figure showing the *pre, post 1* and *post 2* tests of video, verbal, and no golf lessons. The higher up on the graph the better your performance.

As you can imagine, the "no lessons" group really didn't change much during the study. They got a little better after a week of solid practice but they did not get noticeably better. This should come as no surprise because it is what happens for most people when the have their normal practice.

The group that got regular lessons actually got a little worse from the pretest to the post-test 1, but then, after the week break they actually got better. The group that got video lessons also got worse to start off. In fact, they were hitting the ball worse than the other groups on the post-test 1. However, after they had time to let the information settle in they showed the most improvement, and by post-test 2 they were the best of all.

The point here is not that everybody should take video lessons. The point is that if you want to change your swing you have to actually *change* your swing, and sometimes this means getting worse before you get better. The same goes for your mindset on the course. Have patience with any change you are making. Most people are not patient enough to let the process happen. They see the negative results like in post-test 1 and bail out instead of sticking with it long enough to get the post-test 2 results. If you give up good for great, you have to make the commitment and stick to it. Half way does not work. Half way will result in you being worse (and more frustrated) than you were in the first place.

GOOD, BAD, WORSE

Not every story turns out to be a success. I'm sure you know someone who never got any better, or the person who wanted to get better so they took lessons and they actually got worse. I have a friend who was a good golfer. He had been between a 7 and 8 handicap for years. He practiced on his own but could never seem to get much better, and as you can imagine he was getting frustrated. So he took a few lessons. Within two months of taking lessons he has changed his handicap by 5 strokes. He is now a 12.

What happened in my friend's case is what happens in a lot of cases. He got off the bus too soon. That's right, he panicked because he thought that the bus would not take him to where they wanted to go, or maybe the bus wasn't taking him in the right direction fast enough. Instead of riding it out and seeing what would happen, he jumped out of the bus and crash landed. Had he ridden it out a bit longer he may have made the changes he needed to improve. Remember, it even took Tiger 18 months working on it full time to make his swing changes. But my friend did not have the appropriate mindset or patience to ride it out, and he is not alone. Like I said, not every story has a fairy tale ending. If it were easy and quick we would all be great golfers. You need courage to succeed. You have to change your mindset from thinking about the immediate results to looking at the trends over the long run. You wouldn't get out of a long term stock the day after you bought it, would you? Generally this does not make sense and if you do it on a regular basis you will lose a lot of money. The same goes with golf lessons. You shouldn't bail out of golf lessons if they don't pay off immediately. Don't look at a golf lesson as a panacea. One lesson does not fix all. Golf lessons are a process.

Just like the river creature, when you let go of good you may hit a few bumps along the way until you get to great. Likewise, when you risk greatness you may take a turn for the worse in the short run. Taking a step back is no cause for alarm. It may mean that you are in the "dip" stage and ready to move forward. Don't bail out in the dip. Those who bail out do so out of fear. As a result, not many people get to greatness because not many people have the courage to ride out the dip.

Even for those who choose greatness there are good days (or weeks) and bad days. This is especially true early on. For many, this is where the frustration starts. They feel like they are getting better and then all of a sudden a high number pops up, or the swing feels out of sync. For most people, these fluctuations make them want to just give up or go back to the old way of doing things. When this happens take strength in knowing that there is a process to complete, and that by keeping your mind in the process you can go from good to great. So when you get frustrated, and you will, remember; if where you are is good enough, you can stop right now, but if you want more take the extra step. If you want to be great you have to be willing to let go of good.

Think of it as if you are learning to hang glide: one of the first things you need to learn to be able to hang glide is to allow yourself to get off the ground. You can't fly and be on the ground at the same time. But if you let go of the ground, there is a chance you will crash, at least early on, but if you never take the chance to fall you will never have the chance to learn. You have to be willing to fall if you are going to learn to fly.

You have to be willing to fall if you are going to learn to fly.

There is a great line about this in the movie Batman Begins. Early in the movie an eight-year-old boy named Bruce Wayne falls into an abandoned well. As you may know, as an adult Bruce becomes Batman, but for now he is just a scared child. When he fell he broke his arm and in this scene his father is carrying him into the house to set the break.

"Why do we fall, Bruce?" his father asks.

"I don't know why we fall," young Bruce Wayne answers.

"We fall, Bruce, so that we can learn to get up," his father says to finish the scene.

On the road to greatness you will fall from time to time. Learn to get up and you will lose your fear of falling. Let go of the rock and let the river take you to greatness.

Key Points

♦ You have to be willing to let go of good if you are going to be great

♦ A step back is a step, not a step in the wrong direction

♦ Have patience with yourself and the process

♦ The only reason to stop working is if you are completely satisfied with where you are

---

You have to be willing to let go of good if you want to be great.

section two:
Tools
for
Learning

Section I provided you with the mindset that you need for efficient learning. You learned that efficient learning requires patience, commitment, and discipline. Understanding the psychology of learning before you are given the tools for efficient learning is important. If you are given a tool without understanding the basic way that the tool should be used the tool will do you little good. A wrench does not work as a screwdriver nor does a screwdriver work well as a wrench. Understanding the purpose and idea behind the tools is what the psychology of learning is all about.

Section II gives you the tools of learning. In this section we will talk about how people generally practice, why they get frustrated when practice does not turn into better golf scores, and how to reverse this trend. Section II gives you the tools and tells you how to use them.

Goldilocks and the Three Bears

> "Hard training, easy combat;
> easy training, hard combat"
>
> **Marshal Suvorov,**
> famous Russian General who understood training

I don't understand why I don't get any better even though I practice.

Why is it that I can hit the ball great on the range but not on the course?

I don't have much time to practice. What is the fastest way to get better?

If you've ever asked any of these questions, you're not alone. These and many other questions have been asked from many a frustrated golfer. The answers all have to do with a simple principle of learning, which in this case can be thought of as *Goldilocks and the Three Bears.* You may remember how Goldilocks was always complaining about the porridge being too hot or too cold, the bed being too hard or too soft, and so on. Well learning is kind of like that. Too much challenge or too little challenge is not good for learning. We need to be challenged just right.

Although this may sound simple, perhaps too simple to work, there is quite a bit of science behind *Goldilocks*. The scientific version of the Goldilocks principle is called the Challenge Point Framework. Dr.

Tim Lee from McMaster University and I developed the basic idea a few years ago. Tim and I spent years researching the most efficient ways for people to learn, and we came up with an idea that greatly increases learning and decreases frustration. We used all this research to create methods of practice that speed up learning an average of two or three times the normal rate, and in one instance, people actually learned more while practicing 80% less than another group! We also found out why people can practice and practice and yet fail to get any better.

The concept behind the method really does relate to *Goldilocks and the Three Bears*. During practice, one of three things happens: (1) We are challenged too much, (2) we are challenged too little or, on the very rare occasion, (3) we are challenged just right. This may sound nice in theory, but what does it mean in real life, or more importantly, what does it mean for golf?

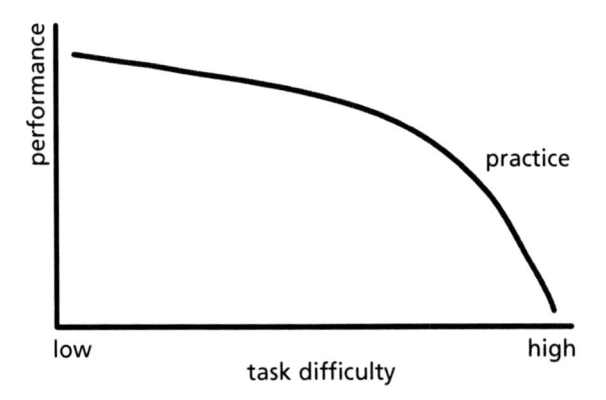

Graph showing how performance during practice gets worse as the task you are practicing becomes more difficult.

Graph reading 101-2: The vertical (y) axis shows performance. In the case of Challenge Point, the performance is how well you are doing on the task. Up on the axis means you are doing well and down means you are doing poorly. The horizontal (x) axis shows scale. In this case it is task difficulty. The further to the right you go the more difficult the task. So if the graph line goes down as it moves to the right, it means that you are worse better as the task gets more difficult. Once again, this is probably straightforward to you but the little reminder will help later on.

The solid line on the graph depicts how task difficulty affects success during practice. In this case, task difficulty is defined simply as the difficulty of the task based on accuracy, coordination, and environment (the circumstances surrounding the task). For example, a 2-foot putt is less difficult than a 20-foot putt. Even if the 2-foot putt makes you feel weak in the knees, the chances of making it are greater than the chances of making a 20-footer. Likewise, trying to hit a driver to a green is more difficult than trying to his a 9-iron to a green. All of these tasks are easier when nothing is on the line. Hitting a 9-iron to a green is easier if you are doing it in practice rather than doing it in front of a crowd at the club championship.

The basic relationship between task difficulty and performance during practice is that as the task difficulty increases, performance decreases. I realize this is not an earth-shattering revelation, but stay with me. If you hit the same 4-foot putt 10 times in a row, you would expect to make the putt seven or eight times. If the task difficulty is increased by changing the putt length from 4 to 10 feet you would expect to struggle a little more. You may only make four or five of the putts. In other words, as practice becomes more difficult, there is greater struggle. This struggle will be something you come to embrace as you go along with this book.

I'll grant you that there is nothing revolutionary about the idea that as the task becomes more difficult you don't do as well, but that is only a small part of the equation for efficient practice, and as it turns out, it is also part of the answer for why people practice the way they do. Specifically, people unwittingly set up practice for success rather than setting up practice for learning. This point will be key as we move through the next few chapters.

People unwittingly set up practice for success rather than setting up practice for learning

Just like in the *Good to Great* chapter, you need to realize that in the short run you may have to give up looking good on the range if you want to play well on the course. Perhaps the best example that I can think of is what Ryan Moore did just before the PGA Championship. It was his rookie year on Tour and he had been plagued with a hand injury. In November of 2005 Ryan fractured a bone in his left hand.

The bone (hook of the hammate) needed to be surgically repaired, but the season wasn't over so Ryan continued to play with the pain. During a conversation with Mark O'Meara at the Honda Classic in Florida, Mark said that he had experienced a similar problem years before and suggested his surgeon, Dr. Jerry Rubin to perform the surgery. Having surgery meant Ryan would have to miss the Masters, arguably his favorite tournament. Not having the surgery meant struggling for the rest of the season and a great deal of pain.

In February 2006 Dr. Rubin performed the surgery. He was a consummate professional. The surgery went well and Dr. Rubin went above and beyond following up with Ryan and his progress. For the next eight weeks Ryan worked diligently at his rehabilitation with a wonderful yet hard driving hand therapist (Kathy Mason). In less than two months Ryan's hand was rehabilitated enough to start hitting balls, albeit with a great deal of pain. He struggled through the first couple of tournaments after he came back because his hand strength was poor and the swing still caused a great deal of pain. Eventually it was discover that only way Ryan could hit balls without a shooting pain was to pre-set his wrist prior to the swing. [If you saw Ryan play in 2006 or his swing sequence in GolfDigest (January, 2007) you know what I am talking about.] It is unconventional to say the least. This discovery was made in May, about 10 weeks after surgery and only a few days before the PGA Championship. In spite of what it looked like on the range Ryan was willing to do it because this is the only way he could practice and prepare for the Championship. As the 2006 Championship got closer Ryan decided that the only way he could hit a ball without a great deal of pain was with the wrist pre-set. He had a choice: He could withdraw from a second major in his rookie year, or play with his 'unconventional' swing. Ryan put pride and appearance aside, addressed the ball, and swung from the hip. Amazingly, he recorded a top 10 (T-9th) in a major using what was called by GolfDigest "The tour's weirdest move."

The goal of your practice should help you make key decisions about how to practice. You practice goal should allow you to easily answer the following questions before you ever go out to practice: Would you rather look good during practice but play poorly, or struggle a little during practice and play well? Do you want to be a driving range player or a tournament player?

WHICH KIND OF PLAYER ARE YOU?

Every year I play in a tournament called Rebel Day. The tournament is a 4-person scramble, with a twist. On each tee is a member of the UNLV golf team. The UNLV golf program is consistently ranked in the top 5 in the country and as you can imagine, it has a stable of very good players. The way the scramble works is that each member of the foursome hits a tee shot. Then, the UNLV golfer hits a tee shot from the same tee. The foursome can use any of the five tee shots as their own. For the UNLV golfer it's just like being on the range, albeit with a lot of time between swings. For the foursomes it's great. I can tell you from personal experience that having collegiate All-Americans hitting tee shots for you makes the foursome look pretty good.

During one of these tournaments, I was paired with a scratch golfer, the father of an LPGA player, and the owner/editor of a golf magazine. My playing partners certainly knew golf, and after each tee shot they couldn't help critiquing the UNLV golfer's swing. Typical comments would be…"What a swing. That guy must be a great player," or, "That's a pretty unconventional swing but it seems to get the job done." Having worked with the UNLV players for years, I had a pretty good understanding of their games. As I listened, it was interesting for me to compare the foursome's comments about the player to the actual success the player had in tournaments. In essence, it was like listening to people predict how well someone was going to score by watching them practice on the driving range. Needless to say, my playing partners were not always accurate in their assessment. As I am sure you have experienced, driving range success does not necessarily predict course success.

REASONS PEOPLE WANT TO HIT
THE BALL WELL ON THE RANGE

Unwittingly, most people set up practice in a way that hinders learning. More than once it has happened that practice on the range one day is much better than performance on the course the next day. This generally happens because people under-challenge themselves on the range (the same goes for the putting green). There are two main reasons this happens. First, most people don't understand that practice performance does not indicate how much they are learning. It is common to think that the better one performs during practice the more one is learning, but as you will see shortly this is simply not the case. The second reason is that ego creeps in now and then.

Next time you go to the driving range before you start hitting balls, just stand back and watch other people on the driving range. If you happen to catch someone who has just hit a bad shot, watch what they do. Almost reflexively they'll look around to see who saw them. It's not that they are an ego-maniac, it's just human nature.

The same thing happens when you're walking along a sidewalk and trip. The first thing you do is look around to see who saw you. I suppose it could be a survival technique that has evolved through generations. You don't want the saber tooth tiger to know you're clumsy because then he will pick you as the target. Just to be on the safe side you look to see if he saw you trip. If he did, you pay special attention to avoid that tiger (and any tiger he has talked to).

In golf circles you might not want your opponents see you 'trip.' Perhaps there is an even simpler reason. Perhaps it is just embarrassing to hit a bad shot and it has nothing to do with survival. Regardless of whether it is an evolutionary response or not, most people don't like looking like they are struggling during practice. However, as soon as you realize that it doesn't help us to make practice easy so we look good, you will be able to put away human nature and become a little more tolerant of a bad shot every now and then. As we will discuss several times in this book, to be successful in golf, you often have to put human nature aside.

Although not related to puppy training, Ben Hogan talked about human nature when he described the golf swing.

PUPPY TRAINING

I remember talking with Ryan about this idea and he told me a story about a new puppy his family had just gotten. In spite of the family's best efforts to train the puppy, it continued to play, chew on shoes, and pee wherever it wanted. Naturally this did not sit well with the family. After a while of watching this Ryan pointed out that what the family was trying to do was train the puppy to not be a puppy. This is a hard thing to do just like it is hard to suppress human nature on the golf course, but unless you want chewed up shoes and bad shots, sometimes you have to go against nature.

"Reverse every natural instinct and do the opposite of what you are inclined to do, and you will probably come very close to having a perfect golf swing." Ben Hogan

To be successful in golf you often have to put human nature aside

One of the ways to take care of this survival/ego issue is to set appropriate practice goals. If you realize that your goal is to learn even if it means struggling, it eases the uncomfortable feeling you get when you hit a bad shot. You can also take care of the ego issue by thinking of your long term goals. We'll talk about goals quite a bit in this book because goals are critical to success. Goals become the roadmap to success. If used correctly, goals direct behavior and allow you to focus on what's important rather than what's immediate. I strongly suggest that each time before you get to the driving range, you write goals for your practice session. Goals such as 'Work on a full shoulder turn,' 'Practice routine for half the swings,' and 'Have fun' all are good reminders, but you can be even more specific by detailing how you are going to have fun or work on the shoulder turn. Chapter 11 will take you through the process of goals, but before we get there let's continue developing tools for learning.

So unless one of your goals is 'Impress others while on the range' your ego should stay out of your practice. Instead, focus on the big prize. Focus on learning so you can take the skills to the course, and learning requires an intelligent struggle.

Learning requires an intelligent struggle

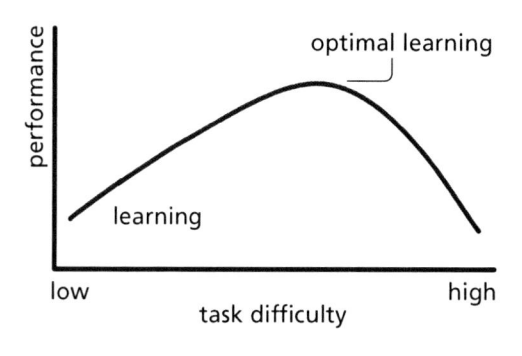

The graph shows what happens with learning as task difficulty increases or decreases. Learning increases as the challenge increases up to a point (optimal learning) and the learning slows and can even stop if the challenge is too great

In this next version of the Challenge Point graph we now have a dotted line. Whereas the last graph showed what happens with practice performance as you increase task difficulty, this graph shows the relationship between task difficulty and *learning*. Learning is measured by how well you do on the course. So when the line goes up, that means that you have better skills to take to the course. Ultimately this will translate into better scores as well.

NO CHALLENGE EQUALS NO LEARNING

There are a couple of interesting points to note about the learning line. First, if task difficulty is low, learning is low. In other words, if the task is too easy you don't learn much. This should be pretty obvious. No challenge equals no learning. So if during practice you hit the same 1-foot straight putt time after time, you won't be much challenged and you won't learn much from it. However, as task difficulty increases, learning increases, at least up to a point. There is a point where you can be challenged too much. Here is where our friend *Goldie Locks* comes back into the picture. Too much challenge or too little challenge is not good. We need just enough challenge. So don't go overboard with the challenge. At this point just realize that a certain amount of challenge is good. To complete the story we need to add the two graphs together.

The first graph showed the relationship between task difficulty and *practice*. The second graph showed the relationship between task difficulty and *learning*. Remember, if the goal is to learn we don't care all that much about practice.

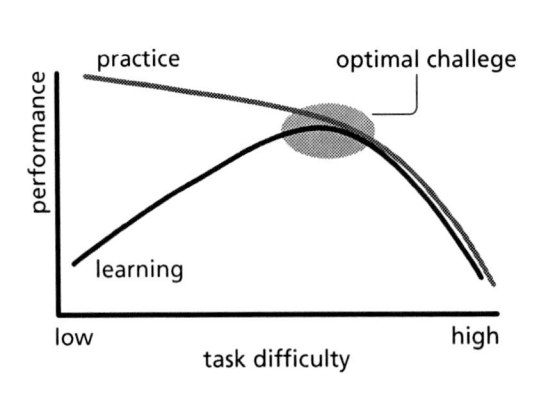

The graph shows what happens with practice and learning as task difficulty increases or decreases. Practice performance decreases and learning increases as the challenge increases up to a point (optimal challenge) and the learning slows and can even stop if the challenge is too great

In this final version of the graph, the solid line again shows the relationship between task difficulty and our success during practice. The dotted line again shows the relationship between task difficulty and our success on the course (learning). When you combine the two lines an interesting relationship emerges. In the beginning, practice performance and learning go in opposite directions as you change task difficulty. With low task difficulty, practice performance is good (solid line) but learning is poor (dotted line). This means that if there is very little task difficulty you may look good during practice but you are not learning much because you are not being challenged. You are training yourself to be a driving range player or a practice green putter.

Low challenge is one of the reasons that you can hit great shots on the practice range but not hit the same great shots on the course

Using the example given earlier, if you hit the same 1-foot straight putt time after time, you'll probably make a lot of the putts, but you won't learn much. Likewise, if you always play from a perfect lie with little consequence for a good or bad shot you may perform well on the range but your learning won't be optimized. However, as task difficulty increases, by increasing the length of the putts, changing the lie, etc., you may not make as many of the putts or hit the ball good every time but you will learn a lot more. As you increase the amount of challenge you increase the amount of learning, at least to a point. The point where the challenge is best for learning is the circle labeled "Optimal Challenge." You have to struggle a bit during practice, but you're learning, and that will translate to better scores on the course.

Good practice performance does not necessarily mean good learning

We're almost done here, but there is one more one piece to the puzzle. How do you know what is optimal practice? How do you know when you are challenging yourself enough without challenging yourself too much? These are great questions. The graphs show the science of learning, but there is an art to learning as well. There needs to be a balance between challenge and success. There also needs to be a balance between ability level and challenge because the same practice will not affect everyone the same way. Matching ability level to challenge is critical. Good teaching pros can help with this, especially those who are not constantly talking during a lesson.

In the next sections we will talk about how to increase and decrease challenge so that you can learn faster and play better.

Throughout this book and there are examples of how to reach the optimal challenge point. In the back section of this book is a worksheet to set up practice for short game and long game so that you have control of your challenge and your success.

Leave your ego home when you go to practice. Struggle on the range so you don't have to struggle on the course.

Reverse Ego

When I was 40 years old, I broke my wrist. I did it while snowboarding. Needless to say, the injury not only hurt my golf game, but it also hurt my ego. When people saw the cast the conversation would go like this.

"Hey, what happened to your arm?"

"I broke my wrist," I would answer, hoping there would be no follow-up. There was always a follow-up.

"How'd you do that?" the question would come.

"Snowboarding," I would answer.

There would be a moment of silence, a curious head tilt and then the *"How dumb are you?"* look. Some of my closer friends skipped the look and just actually asked, *"How dumb are you?"*

If you have ever had such an injury, you know that it takes a long time to recover. For me it was more than a year. The injury happened in January and I couldn't swing a club pain-free until the following January. Because I wanted to make up for lost time, I tried to practice whenever I could. Unfortunately, the months between February and June are very busy working with players and it allowed very little time to practice or play. As a result, I didn't even bring my clubs to the tournaments when I was working.

So as I mentioned, I wanted to make up for lost time but rarely had my clubs. Fortunately, the players with whom I was working would let me use their clubs, and this is where Reverse Ego comes in. I would take the clubs to the most out of the way place on the driving range. I would warm up and start hitting balls. I can tell you that it was not pretty. One day when I was hitting, a group of spectators slowly started working their way down to me. I didn't notice at first. I was hitting for about 5-10 minutes before I even looked back. There they were, watching me hit balls.

Why would they watch me? Because they thought they were watching the person whose bag I was using. They saw the name on the bag and assumed I was a in the tournament. As soon as I realized this I felt bad for the player. Here are these people watching what they think is a tournament player hit some horrendous shots. I went to the player and confessed what had happened. Rather than being upset, he laughed. He wasn't the least bit bothered by what people thought of 'his' driving range performance. He understood that no driving range performance ever won a golf tournament. Incidentally the player whose clubs I used won the tournament. Those people watching must have thought he had the greatest short game in the world.

Key Points

♦ Practice performance does not tell us how much we are learning.

♦ Put away ego on the range to optimize performance on the course.

♦ Set goals for practice and commit to them.

♦ Good shots on the range do not guarantee good shots on the course.

Pay Now or Pay Later

> "Unhappiness results when we trade what we want most for what we want at the moment."
>
> **Thomas Monson**

THE WHY AND HOW OF PRACTICE

So you buy into the idea that a little struggle during practice is good for you, but how do you do it? How should you practice? Certainly there are good ways and bad ways to practice. I'm sure you've had times when you practice but don't seem to get any better and other times when practice works like a charm. Rather than leaving it up to chance you can put science to work for you to dramatically increase your odds of success. The science of practice is what follows in this book. Practice science can help you get the most out of each practice session and if you follow what is laid out for you, it will dramatically speed your learning and decrease your frustration.

The first thing you need to understand is that ways to practice run along a continuum. By continuum I am talking about a range or scale. Take for example the attribute of beauty. At one end of the continuum is strikingly beautiful and at the other end is butt ugly (each defined in the eye of the beholder). Most people are going to fall along the continuum somewhere between beautiful and ugly. Rarely is someone going to be purely beautiful or purely ugly. Practice is the same way but now rather than beautiful and ugly the ends of the practice continuum are *elaborative practice* and *repetitive practice.*

Before I define what these types of practice are, you need to know that repetitive practice creates weak memories, and you generally do not want weak memories. Elaborative practice creates strong memories. If you want to learn you want to have strong memories. Intuition should tell you that strong memories are remembered and weak ones are not. How you make strong or weak memories is the trick. How well you learn is dictated by *how well* you practice, not *how much* you practice and this simple fact can dramatically change the way most golfers practice.

Practice does not always equal learning

REPETITIVE PRACTICE

Let's say that you happen to be in Emporia (Kansas) for a business trip. You are in your hotel room and you want to order a pizza. So you take out the telephone book and look up the number for a pizza place, and you repeat it to yourself a few times as you walk to the telephone to dial. Once you have dialed and start to talk, you forget the number. In a way, the fact that you so easily forgot the number makes for a great memory system. It may sound odd but it's true. The system that just lets that number slip out of your memory is great. Why would a system that doesn't hold information in memory be great?

Think of your memory as a computer. If you saved every file, every version, every email, everything you worked on, things would get pretty crowded. Now, if you were looking for a particular file and you had to wade through the tens of thousands of other files on your hard drive, think of how long it would take to look for it. On the other hand, think of a situation where the computer knew what to keep and what to throw away? You didn't have to ask the computer to save a file and you didn't have to ask the computer to trash a file. The computer just knew what to do. That would be a great system, and in fact, that is the system you have built into your brain. If you remembered everything your brain would be cluttered with lots of useless information, and I'm not talking about the good useless information that helps with Trivial Pursuit. Anytime you needed important information you would have to look through the clutter.

There is really no reason to remember the telephone number of a pizza place in Emporia if you never plan to be there again. Your brain knows this and so it has a system to forget. This system is called repetitive practice (aka rote practice), and it is the same system people use when they practice golf.

Since you are smart and keeping up, you know that it doesn't make sense to use repetitive practice for golf. After all, repetitive practice is designed so that information is only remembered for a short amount of time, and then it is wiped away so it won't clutter up your brain. If you think about how most people hit balls on the range, you can see that it is just like repeating the telephone number to yourself time after time. Next time you go to a driving range, notice how people are practicing. They will take a single club time after time. Hit a ball, scrape another one from the pile right away, and hit that one. Hit and scrape. Hit and scrape. Most people don't even wait for the first ball to finish rolling before they are scraping another ball from the pile. Even though they are practicing, they probably are not learning, at least not very well.

Like the situation with the telephone number, just because you repeat information doesn't mean you remember it. I've had many people tell me that they practice and practice and just don't seem to get better. When I observe how they practice most of these people use repetitive practice on the range. If you have this problem you may wonder what to do about it. Simple, go to the other end of the continuum and let elaborative practice come to your rescue!

"Repetition" does not always equal "Remembering"

ELABORATIVE PRACTICE

Elaborative practice, as the name implies, means to elaborate, or think about each practice trial. Generally, elaborative practice requires conscious thought and time, but it is well worth it because in the long run a little thought can save you a lot of time and frustration.

When I was a kid I had to learn a new telephone number, and the last four digits were 3312. I could have just practiced saying 3312 over and over again and hope that after hundreds times I would remember it. But I didn't have the patience to practice hundred of times, nor did my parents have the patience to listen to me. Instead, they suggested that I use elaborative practice as a way to remember the number. They gave me one little trick and I learned the new telephone number in *one trial!* How is this possible?

It was the mid-1970s when I had to learn the new telephone number. At the time the new number was not important to me. In fact, as a young boy growing up in Dallas few things in my life were important other than the Dallas Cowboys. As you might know, the 1970s Dallas Cowboys were America's team, after all. (I'd rather not talk about what has happened to my beloved Cowboys since then.) Two of my favorite Cowboys were Tony Dorsett and Roger Staubach. As it turns out, Tony Dorsett's jersey number was 33, and Roger Staubach's number was 12. All I had to do was remember Dorsett and Staubach and I knew the number. Since I already knew their jersey numbers (and the numbers of every other player on the team), once I connected them to my new telephone number, I had it. Very little time on my part and some creativity on my parents' part saved all of us a lot of frustration. Just think of how much frustration elaborative practice could save you.

By the way, obviously my parents didn't invent elaborative practice. It has been around for centuries. In fact, many of the 'memory tricks' that you are taught to remember someone's name, a list for the grocery store, etc. are nothing more than elaborative practice. Next time you meet someone new, try to think of a person you already know with the same name and you will have it. If it is a unique name and you don't know anyone with that name to tie it to you have to be creative. Say you meet a girl whose name is 'Mits.' Perhaps you can think of how it reminds you of a particularly outstanding anatomical feature. Regardless of your connection, elaboration is a powerful tool, and it is generally the way you should practice golf.

> ### A golf example of elaborative practice:
> I have several common swing flaws. One of my swing flaws is taking the club past parallel at the top of my swing. I thought it was because I was over-swinging, so I practiced having less turn. It just didn't seem to work. One day, I thought I would spend a little time in elaborative practice. I imagined what position I wanted at the top of my swing. The position was very similar to how I used to hold a tray when I was a waiter (many years ago). I decided that a key to my top position was holding a tray like a waiter. So I positioned my right hand like a waiter holding a tray, then placed the club in my hand, put my left hand on the club, and I had the position. That few seconds taught me more about correct position than an hour of hitting balls without direction.

Elaborative practice works because it gets information deeper into memory by connecting what we are trying to learn with something we already know. Elaborative practice is a "rich get richer" scheme if you use it right. The more you know, the easier it is to learn.

Living in Las Vegas and having taught this idea to many college students, the analogy of a doorman at an ultra-popular nightclub comes to mind. In Las Vegas, the popular nightclubs all have lines to get in. Sometimes the lines reach a few hundred people, and the only way in is through the doorman. He is the gatekeeper. If you either know the doorman or you can make a connection  with him, the chances of getting in are pretty good, otherwise you may have a long and frustrating wait.

If you don't know the doorman you have some choices to make. You can show up in line every night and stand there with little effort to make a connection. This is like repetitive practice. Even though you keep repeating the process the chances of getting in are not great because there is no connection. On the other hand, you can get to know the doorman by putting some thought into the process. Develop a good plan. Find out what is meaningful to him and use that information. If you can't get to the doorman directly, get to know someone who knows him and let that be your bridge. These methods may take a little creativity, but it will be well worth the effort.

In the golf world, this means if you practice for one hour without meaning you just wasted an hour of your time. On the other hand, if you can connect meaning to what you are trying to learn, you have a good chance of learning it. If you can't do it yourself have someone who already knows the information (like a teaching pro) help you get to know it. Just like the doorman, you either make the connection yourself or have someone help you make the connection, otherwise you will be waiting for a long time to get where you want to go.

Either make the connection yourself or have someone help you make the connection

> *Remember,* there are three probable reasons people set up practice using repetition.
>
> 1. They don't realize that easy practice means a hard time on the course
>
> 2. Repetition is easier than elaborative practice and people are very efficient (or lazy)
>
> 3. Ego gets in the way because proper goals have not been set

SUMMARY

If you try to go for shortcuts, you will short cut yourself. Pay now in the form of a little extra effort so you won't have to pay later in frustration. Use the fact that learning is a "rich get richer" scheme to your advantage. The more you know, the easier it is to learn. For example, if you have a background in accounting, it will be easier for you to learn new accounting rules than it would be for someone who has no accounting background. Likewise, the more you know about golf, the easier it is for you to understand new information about golf. As such, a little extra effort now pays off in dividends as you learn. The more you can make connections between what you know and what you are trying to learn, the easier it will be to make connections in the future. If you use a little thought (elaborative practice), you will learn much faster than if you just bang balls with no real purpose (repetitive practice).

Elaborative practice requires conscious thought. Elaborative practice requires more effort than repetitive practice, and that's why it works. Elaborative practice engages your brain. Regardless of what you have heard about 'muscle memory,' it is your brain that learns, not your muscles. Your muscles are the tools of the brain. Again, using the example of the doorman, if you just stand in line every night, your chances of getting in quickly are not good. However, if you give it a little thought, and learn to connect with him, over time your chances will improve dramatically. Taking this example to the practice range, what I'm saying is that by taking the time to develop meaning for what you're doing on the practice tee, your chances of learning will improve dramatically.

The next chapters explain how to know the doorman. It takes a little effort and a little time, and it is not always as obvious as you may think, but it is well worth the effort in the long run. So you have a choice: You can pay now or pay later. Pay now with the time and effort of elaborative practice, and receive better golf in the long run. Pay later with repetitive practice. It is easy to do but in return for taking the easy route you have to pay later with frustration and lack of improvement. Believe me; it is much better to pay now for riches later.

> ### *Key Points*
>
> ♦ Repetitive practice is shallow practice - BAD
>
> ♦ Elaborative is deep practice - GOOD
>
> ♦ Pay now or pay later, you have a choice, it's your choice

Feedback is our Friend

> "The trouble with practice is that when you do it, you only practice what you are practicing, not what you may think you are practicing. Practicing bad motions does not build good skills."
>
> *-McCluggage*

As you will see shortly, there are many ways to go about elaborative practice, but each way has two things in common: they allow time for the memory to develop and they attach meaning. Both aspects are important to get information into long-term memory. The three sections that follow describe the best ways to create elaborative practice. The first is related to feedback. The second is related to time, and the third details an "automatic" way to learn. However, don't jump the gun here by going straight to the automatic way of learning. Everything needs to happen in its time. Use sections one and two as a road map to the third section.

TYPES OF FEEDBACK

In its simplest form you can think of feedback as information, and there are two basic sources for this information. You can get feedback on your own or you can get feedback from another source. For example, after you do a presentation you have a general idea of how you did but you can get additional feedback from someone at the presentation. When you get feedback on your own it is called experiential feedback, because it is feedback you give yourself based on your experience. When you get feedback from a source other than yourself (e.g. coach) it is called instructional feedback because it is used to instruct you as to what you did well and what you can improve. The interplay between these two types of feedback is critical for efficient learning and it is a place many people make a mistake both when they get lessons and when they practice on their own.

Now that you understand the basic types of feedback let's take it to the golf world. The ball flight, the click of a shot, and the feel of your body as you hit the ball are all considered experiential feedback. (In the scientific world this type of feedback is known as proprioception.). The better you are the more you can and should rely on experiential feedback. However, sometimes you need help understanding what is going on, and this is where you can use instructional feedback.

> ### *WHEN PROPRIOCEPTION DOESN'T GO AS PLANNED*
> For the first 19 years of his life Ian Waterman, like most everyone else, thought little about his ability to sense the position and movement of his body. All this ended when Waterman suffered a viral infection that destroyed the nerves responsible for his proprioception as well as those for feeling light touch. Although he had full movement, he lost all feeling below the neck. As a result he was unable to tell how what position his body or limbs were in unless he looked. That was 1972 and even Waterman's doctors had a hard time understanding the extent of his disability. Through years of trial and error, Waterman taught himself how to move again by visually monitoring every action. That is, the only way he knew how to move was by seeing his limbs moving. This would be the equivalent of having to watch your entire golf swing to hit the ball. See if you can hit a ball that way.

In golf, instructional feedback generally comes from a teacher, coach, video camera, etc. You need this type of feedback if you don't know exactly what is wrong with your game. The less you know about golf the more you need instructional feedback. However, as your game improves you should transfer from instructional feedback to experiential feedback. In fact, the goal of any good teacher should be to teach you to know and understand your own swing, and your game, not just teach you his or her method. This way, on the course you rely not on what you were taught, but on what you know. This idea was first brought to me by Mike Moore (Ryan's father and teacher) who said, *"Although you are not an island unto yourself on the practice ground, you certainly are on the course."*

The natural question is if we have experiential feedback why do we need instructional feedback? Can't you just figure out the swing by yourself? Remember the quote from McCluggage at the beginning of the chapter? You learn what you are practicing, so if you are practicing the wrong thing you are learning the wrong thing. If your experiential feedback is not accurate you will not be learning what you think you are learning.

A good friend of mine is a golf pro at a very nice club in Las Vegas. He and I were on the range together hitting balls and he couldn't help himself from commenting on a noticeable flaw in my swing. He told me that I dipped my left shoulder when I started the club back (which resulted in becoming too steep in my turn and a loss of power that a good shoulder turn produces). Of course I knew he was wrong because I don't dip my shoulder. That is, I knew he was wrong until he showed me my swing on video. My experiential feedback was wrong because I had trained myself to believe that the feeling of dipping my shoulder was not actually dipping my shoulder. To fix this problem I had to retrain myself. To keep from dipping my shoulder I actually had to feel that I was raising my shoulder as I started the club back. As anyone who has tried to improve their golf swing can attest, retraining bad habits is much more difficult than learning from scratch. The reason for this is that we have preconceived notions of how to interpret certain experiential feedback (proprioception) and what those interpretations mean as far as our golf swing.

On a nearly daily basis we assume certain things about movement and only when something goes awry do we notice the need for retraining. If you have ever used a treadmill you have experienced retraining. Run or walk for 20-30 minutes on a treadmill and when you get off and walk on the ground you will feel an odd sensation. You may feel that you are moving at a faster pace than normal. The reason for this is that you have been retraining your feedback system. For 30 minutes, your senses have been telling you that moving your legs in a walking fashion does not make you move forward. Then, when you get off the treadmill and start to walk on the ground, the same walking motion makes you move forward. Relatively speaking, the world is moving by you much faster than it was only a short while ago when you were on the treadmill.

Another example of inaccurate senses is "sea legs." When you are on a boat, most of your senses tell your body that you are on solid ground (because the deck underneath you is solid, but your inner ear knows better). However, the 'ground' is actually moving up and down with the waves. After a while your body will train itself that the up and down movement is stable. Then, when you get on land, the stable ground will feel like it is moving down and up – the opposite of the boat.

The treadmill and sea legs are very similar to what happened to me when I inaccurately interpreted my shoulder to be level when in fact it was moving down. Because I knew dipping your shoulder isn't good I had trained my senses that the dipping motion felt like a turning motion. To correct this I had to retrain myself by feeling that my shoulder was moving up. You may have had a similar experience when someone helps you with alignment. If you are told that you are open to the target and then you get properly aligned (square) to the target, you will feel closed. This is because you have been telling yourself for some time that a certain feeling and look is square to the target. You have drawn a relationship between a feeling and a position, but the relationship is inaccurate. To correct this, you must reset your equilibrium point, which will reset your senses. We'll talk about how to reset the equilibrium point a bit later.

So the question is how do you retrain your senses so that everything works the way you want it to? The answer is that you need a different type of feedback, and there is no time to waste. The more you practice with the old methods and old relationship between your body and your senses, the more you will ingrain bad habits. This is one reason that practicing without good feedback is a bad thing. To do it right you need to get an accurate source of feedback and start retraining your senses.

Practice doesn't make perfect. Practice makes permanent so you better be practicing the right thing.

The new source of feedback you need generally comes from a teacher, coach, mirror, or video camera. For example, if you are trying to change your swing plane, it is helpful to have a teacher and/or video camera with you. You and your teacher can use the video to see example swings of you and other players, and the same video can document the changes made during the lesson or between lessons. The video can also be used later during practice to remind you of the lessons and to see if you are successful in what you are trying to change. The extra set of eyes, be they human or electronic, can tell you what you are actually doing rather than what you think you are doing. Remember, the mind can play tricks when interpreting the senses.

If you're like me, you'll be surprised to see what your swing looks like for the first time on video. Oftentimes seeing your swing on video is like hearing your voice on a tape recording. When you hear your voice your first thought might be, "I don't sound like that." The truth is that for better or worse you do sound like that. The recording doesn't lie. The same thing may happen when you see a video of your swing. It's not necessarily that your swing is bad; in fact you may be pleasantly surprised at the good parts of your swing or tempo. Good or bad, one reason we are often surprised by tapes is that our senses are fallible, which is precisely the point. To train correctly, you need an accurate and reliable source of information.

You need an accurate and reliable source of information

HOW MUCH IS ENOUGH?

Fortunately, science, technology, and the skilled teacher can combine to provide the right type and right amount of feedback for the most efficient learning. Also fortunately, you already have an idea of how to retrain your senses because it all relates back to the Challenge Point theory discussed earlier. Hopefully you will remember that Challenge Point theory is like Goldilocks; too much is no good. Too little or too much is no good, but just the right amount is just right.

For years now my colleagues and I have studied how feedback affects our ability to learn, and we've developed a few basic guidelines that help with learning. These basic guidelines can make the retraining of old skills or the learning of new skills many times faster. For instructional feedback:

#1. Telling you often you what you need to do and how to do it will generally help you perform better during practice, but this is not necessarily a good thing. For example, you are having a lesson with a pro and every 2-3 swings he tells you how to correct your swing. Presuming you can implement what he is suggesting, you will be able to hit a lot of good shots while you on the range. Don't get too excited about this. Remember the goal of practice is to learn for the course, not just to perform well on the range. In other words, immediate improvement is less important than long-term improvement on the course.

#2. Giving you feedback often during practice may hurt you on the course. If you get frequent feedback during practice you may come to rely on this feedback and when you coach isn't with you on the course you may feel lost. This is why I believe that a good teacher should help you to know and understand your own swing. The good teacher will help you transition between instructional feedback and experiential feedback and constantly telling you what to do is generally not the best way to do this.

At this point you may be asking the question *What is the best way to get feedback?* The answer is that it depends (I know, my students hate that answer as well). It depends on how good you are and what you are trying to learn. It depends on Goldilocks because feedback, like most aspects of practice, is not a one-size-fits-all proposition.

Feedback is not a one-size-fits-all proposition

Several times in the following paragraphs I will make the point that feedback has to be adjusted to the individual for efficient learning. This may sound obvious when you read it, but in fact most people generally want too much information and they want it too often, regardless of their skill level. Silence, especially during a lesson, causes some people distress. In fact, this is one time where silence might be golden, at least in moderation.

As chance would have it I was at the Congressional Country Club in Bethesda, Maryland. It is an absolutely beautiful club and since it was built in 1924 it has been the home of many of the great movers and shakers in U.S. politics. I was there to work Ryan Moore as he played a practice round just between tournaments. As is common we were paired with one of the club's members. This gentleman was an extremely accomplished business man who regularly played with former U.S. presidents and high members of Congress. He was also an excellent golfer, having qualified for the U.S. Senior Amateur several times. During the round he was playing quite well but wanted some advice on how to improve his swing. Like most good golfers he was a perfectionist. He asked if Ryan and I would watch him after the round was over and give advice if we had any.

Ryan and I have a similar philosophy when it comes to helping out with a swing, especially with good players. Watch and learn, and comment sparingly. As such, we watched him hit balls for about three minutes, one of us made a comment about hip movement, and watched for about three or four more minutes. At this point we had only made one comment in six or seven minutes of hitting balls. As he kept hitting ball I could tell that the comment about hip movement was starting to take effect and his ball flight was changing in the correct direction. I also got the sense that the silence was making our new friend uncomfortable, so I asked him to stop hitting balls and then asked why he seemed so uncomfortable. He explained that he didn't understand why we weren't talking to him, and in fact he had just has a series of lessons (away from Congressional) that had been fashioned like ongoing conversations while he hit balls.

"Did you improve from those lessons?" I asked.

"Yes, I hit the ball great," he responded.

"Do you mean that you hit the ball great during the lessons or the next week on the course?" I asked.

At this, contemplation fell over him, shortly followed by an epiphany. *"Come to think of it, I hit the ball great during the lessons but I had a hard time taking the things we talked about to the course. I found myself trying to remember what we had talked about during the lessons."*

"If your goal is hitting the ball well during the lessons I will

talk to you as much as you want, but if your goal is better play I'll need you to trust me a little."

I heard from him after the U.S. Senior Amateur and he said much of what we had worked on had stuck. Infrequent feedback worked because the man was such a good player. The Challenge Point theory presented in Chapter 5 states that there is an optimal point at which people should be challenged. If he was not such a good player I would have changed the frequency with which I gave him feedback. The point is that there is a specific amount of feedback one should be given to learn most efficiently, and this amount is dictated by the skill level of the individual.

The graph below is similar to ones shown earlier, high versus low handicappers, except now feedback frequency is varied. High feedback frequency means that instructional feedback is given often, perhaps every 2-3 shots. Low frequency means that feedback is given infrequently, perhaps every 10-15 shots. Every 20 shots may seem like a lot but we have data that shows such infrequent feedback can be good for the expert performer. As you would guess, the actual frequency depends on the ability level of the golfer and what he is working on.

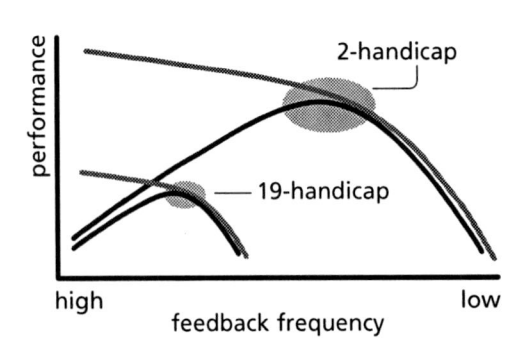

The circles show the optimal level of feedback for the high and low handicappers. High (frequent feedback) is best for the 19-handicapper's learning but that would be too much feedback for the 2-handicapper. Less frequent feedback works better for the better player.

Just like the last time Challenge Point was discussed, the same basic curve exists between performance and learning. In this case, less feedback means more challenge. More specifically, by less I mean less often, or less frequently. Another way to think of this is that feedback provides guidance, and some guidance is good but too much is bad. For example, you fly into Las Vegas and need to get from the airport to the Shadow Creek golf course. It's a great golf course, by the way. You pick up a rental car and since I know how to get to Shadow Creek you ask if I could go along. The course is about 18.5 miles from the airport and to get there you will have to negotiate several surface streets and a highway. I agree to help but I am not going to do it by giving directions. Instead, I am going to give you driving feedback, the equivalent of instructional feedback. I could go about this two ways.

> **Method 1:** I give you information every step along the way. I tell you how far until the next turn, what to look for along the way, when to turn and in what direction to turn. Basically I am your GPS system.

> **Method 2:** I only give you feedback every two minutes. If, along the way, you missed a turn, you would have to go back to correct yourself.

Which method is best for you? It depends on your knowledge of the city and what you want to accomplish. If you are new to the city, you are not interested in learning the streets of the city, and/or your goal is simply to get to Shadow Creek, Method 1 is definitely your best bet. You will make no mistakes, it will be easy, and you will get to the course efficiently. However, you will have no idea how to get back to the airport and if you ever have a chance to play Shadow Creek again you will need directions. In other words, Method 1 was easy but you didn't learn much. On the other hand, if you have some knowledge of the city and you want to learn to navigate the streets even better and you actually want to be able to get to Shadow Creek on your own sometime, Method 2 is best for you. The delayed feedback will make you figure it out yourself. You will have to struggle a bit but in just two or three trips you will know how to get there. Feedback in golf works the same way.

According to Challenge Point, the more expertise you have, the more you should work out the answers on your own. For the 2-handicapper, the optimal challenge point is toward the low feedback (right) side of the graph. The 2-handicapper basically knows what is going on with his swing and only occasionally needs outside information. Just like in the driving example, the struggle of figuring it out is part of the learning equation. In other words, the 2-handicapper has good experiential feedback and only needs a little instructional feedback to fine tune the system. On the other hand, the 19-handicapper does not have good experiential feedback and therefore needs a lot of instructional feedback to tune the system. Therefore, the same occasional feedback that the 2-handicapper gets would not work well for the 19-handicapper.

In the driving example, the person unfamiliar with the city doesn't even know which direction to start. Likewise, the 19-handicapper does not know what is wrong with his swing nor does he know what swing thoughts and feelings he should have. It would be very difficult for the 19-handicapper to bring about positive change without having enough information. For the 19-handicapper, the optimal challenge point is toward the high frequency (left) side of the graph.

In the case of both the 2-handicapper and the 19-handicapper the shapes of the curves look the same. Learning is optimized where practice performance is appropriately challenging. The only difference is at what point of feedback the appropriate challenge comes.

Learning is optimized when practice is appropriately challenging

A GOLF EXAMPLE OF HOW THIS WORKS

You are a 19-handicapper and you have been playing golf for about 10 years. You have decided you want to get down to a 10-12 so you need to change your swing. At first, you will need instructional feedback every 2-3 shots. This may seem a bit overwhelming in the beginning because you will be getting so much feedback. However, your old habits are strong and you need constant reinforcement to change them. Additionally, you do not have the same memory base as a top player and so you don't have the same frame of reference to change your swing.

In general the less skilled you are, the more frequently you need feedback. However,

When people think of frequent feedback there is a tendency to interpret this as a lot of feedback, which in turn can mean feedback about a lot of things. In fact, what I mean by frequent feedback, especially for higher handicappers, is feedback about the same thing but on a regular basis. For example, if you are working on shoulder turn, feedback should only be given about shoulder turn. Too much of anything, even a good thing, can compromise the goal.

be careful with this. Regardless of your level you can overdo the feedback. You still need time to think and digest the information so you don't want your teacher to be constantly chattering away about your swing. You will leave the lesson worn out and confused. Make sure your teacher gives you one point at a time. Work on that before you move to another point. If you have more than two or three items to work on per lesson, you have too many. The basic rule of thumb is that the more of a novice you are, the easier it is to overwhelm the system. The KISS (Keep it Simple Stupid) principle works here, but the KISS should be frequent. You need a few swings, say two or three, with the new information, then feedback about one thing, then a few more swings with the same talking points, and so on until the basic skill you are trying to achieve is fairly automatic.

Now, let's say you are a 2-handicapper. Under this scenario the picture is quite different. A lot of feedback during practice may help your practice performance but it will actually hurt your learning. In this case, you should get very little feedback from your teacher. Otherwise you will hit the ball well during practice but you may actually take a step back on the course. This can cause frustration and may cause you to retreat back to your old ways.

> I knew a player who had been brought up with lessons his whole life. The kid practically lived at a teaching facility. He was the essence of technical perfection. When he moved away from home and went to play in college he no longer had constant lessons. Soon, a few things started to go wrong with his swing as they do with most any swing. The problem was that he had no idea how to fix them. For years he had been trained how to listen to a teacher. He had not been trained on the golf swing. He was given too much feedback and had become dependent on it. Even too much of a good thing can be bad.

The reason that the amount of feedback needs to be tailored for each player is that each player is different. I know this sounds obvious but I can assure you some teachers give lessons as a one-size-fits-all proposition. Even if you are looking in a mirror or a video camera, you need to realize that the feedback changes as you change. This idea is squarely founded on the Challenge Point theory.

If you are a high handicapper, too little feedback is too much challenge.

You need more guidance as you are trying to change your swing and learn how to interpret the messages coming from your senses. If you are a low handicapper, too much feedback is not enough challenge. Too much feedback will be like taking you by the hand and walking you through the swing. This may be great for practice but you will be lost when you go to the course. You will have too many thoughts running through your head rather than taking your time and letting the information sink in. As a result you will be trying to remember what the teacher talked about rather than letting the swing just happen. Too many thoughts can ruin any swing.

The challenge has to match the performer

Low handicappers usually only need tweaks when they practice or get lessons, and they have a good sense of what their body is doing. Even though it might not be comfortable during a lesson, the brain of the low handicapper thrives on more challenge. If you are a low handicapper you can and should figure out some things on your own. In fact, the better the player you are, the less you should get feedback and the more you should give it. Ideally, a very good golfer will tell the pro what is going on with the swing rather than have the pro tell him. The pro can confirm or deny what you think you are doing. This way, you are not only tweaking the swing to make it even sounder, you are also learning about the swing rather than having everything handed to you. On the course this will pay off for you many times over. This type of practice is more difficult, but the challenge is exactly what makes the learning efficient.

The focus of Challenge Point as it relates to feedback is that you should apply as much challenge as a player can handle. It may make practice a little difficult but it will really help learning and as such it will create better golf on the course.

The better you are, the less feedback you should be given

Now that you know the basics of feedback, we can take this information and create learning schedule that works. As with all the examples used in this section, there are examples of full swing and putting. Pay attention to the similarities and differences between the examples. There are some fundamental truths about feedback and elaborative practice, and that's where you will see the similarities. There are also some adjustments that need to be made for efficient practice and these adjustments make up the differences you will notice.

> ### *SUMMARY*
>
> ♦ Feedback can come from a teacher, coach, knowledgeable friend, or video camera.
>
> ♦ Match the amount of feedback to the level of expertise. The better golfer you are, the less feedback you should have.
>
> ♦ This means the scratch player should go 10-15 shots before given feedback whereas the 20-handicap should get feedback every 4-5 shots.

Examples of FEEDBACK during practice

Anything related to feedback is greatly facilitated by a coach or teacher because they are your accurate source of information. This is particularly important for golfers just learning the game because as I mentioned before, the golf senses are not well developed for novice golfers. As such, I strongly advise getting lessons if you are just starting out. I actually advise getting lessons regardless of your expertise, but if you are little more advanced you can stumble through without lessons, it just may not be pretty. Regardless of whether or not you get a coach, know that appropriate feedback during practice can speed learning 3-5 times faster than doing it on your own.

NOTE: *Some people prefer not to go to a PGA Professional (i.e., teacher) at all, and most people, even if they do have a teacher, practice without a teacher most of the time. For these people, use the example below, but rather than using a teacher as your source of feedback, use a video camera.*

Full swing (1 hour)

Regardless of your level of expertise, you can only handle so much information. So for all types of practice it is best to organize practice into sections. In fact, if all you do is organize practice into sections and set a plan (what will later be called a GPA) for each practice session, you are ahead of the game.

In this example you have an hour to practice full swing. After warm up, take 5 minutes working on tempo by hitting ½ shots and ¾ shots with a wedge. During this first section of practice, you are not trying to learn the swing as much as you are trying to establish tempo. A consistent tempo is important for a consistent swing. One simple way to carry out a tempo drill is just to talk during the swing. Talk to a practice partner or to yourself (out loud). It is hard to talk and swing if you don't have good tempo. Additionally, any part of your swing that is not automatic will suffer if you talk through it and so this will be good feedback for you. If you are with a coach, their job at this point is to observe your set up and swing.

When you are actually ready for full swings, ask your teacher to watch you swing without a ball. Since most teachers use video technology now, you can record a couple of swings with a ball and a couple without a ball. That way you will be able to see if your swing changes as a result of the ball. You'd be surprised at how many players change their swing from their practice (without a ball) to the actual swing (with a ball). If the ball changes your swing this tells you that part of your problem with your swing may be mental rather than physical. I don't mean that you're a nut job. I mean that something about having to contact the ball changes your ability to swing the golf club. Believe me; this is more common than you may think.

Once you have demonstrated your basic swing for your teacher, it's time to get to work. Each teacher has their method of what they like to work on and how, but you can control a great deal of the pace of the lesson. Specifically, you can control the amount of feedback you get during a lesson. The basic rule is this: The better you are, the less feedback you should get from the teacher, but when you do get feedback it should be very specific. Appropriate feedback for the experienced golf might be "You took the club away too much inside". Likewise, the more novice you are, the more feedback you should get from the teacher, but when you do get feedback it should be very general. Appropriate feedback for the novice golf might be "You lifted your head too much".

A low handicapper should get feedback every 10-15 shots. A midrange player (10-15 handicap) should get feedback every 4-5 shots. A novice golfer should get feedback 2-3 shots. Many very good pros know this, but don't take it for granted. You can help the process along by asking for feedback when you need it and asking for no feedback when you don't. Part of the process of learning is understanding when and how much you need to struggle in figuring out the golf swing. This is one of the important ideas behind Challenge Point. If you are able to get to a point where you can work efficiently on your own when you are practicing, you will be able to work on your own on the course. If you find that your teacher is giving you too much feedback, simply ask them to stop for a few shots. This way, you work with the teacher rather than having the teacher do all the work. This will reap dividends when the teacher is no longer there, like during a round of golf.

You can combine feedback and elaboration by working your clubs up and down, hitting a few shots with one club then switching clubs. The same rules of feedback apply. The extent to which you switch clubs is based on what you are working on that day and your level of expertise. As a general rule, the more advanced you are, the more you can switch clubs. The less advanced you are, the less you should switch clubs.

The reason for this is the Challenge Point. If you don't have a consistent swing, you don't want to change too many things at once. That would be too much challenge. Keep the club consistent if your swing is inconsistent, and keep the clubs inconsistent if your swing is consistent. For the medium to experienced golfer, each time you switch clubs you should take a break. Remember, we can only digest so much information at a time. If you have a teacher talking to you for an hour straight while you are hitting and while you are not hitting, that is just too much to handle.

I would recommend that you take at least two minutes off every 15 minutes during a lesson. This would mean that you have a 5-minute tempo session, then 15 minutes of lessons, then 2 minutes off, 15 minutes on, 2 minutes off, 15 minutes on, 2 minutes off, and 10 minutes on. During this last 10-minute session, give yourself a test. With your teacher watching, hit shots while working on what you learned that day, but ask the teacher not to comment until you are finished. Then, hit the last few shots, ask your teacher to watch to see what you have learned and give you final pointers. By the way, those 6 minutes that you take off during an hour practice are absolutely worth it. That time will decrease mental fatigue, decrease confusion, and as we will talk later, it will give your brain time to digest the information you are trying to learn. Likewise, immediately after the lesson you should write notes about what you learned as a reminder to you and to check that you understood everything.

  Unfortunately, most average golfers do not get putting lessons. This is not the case for high-level golfers, including professionals. They take care to work on putting just like the full swing. If you want to play like the professionals you should do what they do. Have a short game coach. The exact same techniques talked about for the full swing can be used for short game. However, for putting, rather than changing clubs you change putts. Other than that, the same rules apply.

> ### Key Points
>
> ♦ You need an accurate and reliable source of information
>
> ♦ The challenge has to match the performer
>
> ♦ The better you are, the less feedback you should be given
>
> ♦ As you increase ability, decrease how often you get feedback
>
> ♦ Learning is optimized where practice performance is appropriately challenging. The difference between beginners and experts is the point at which feedback creates an appropriate challenge.

Time is on Your Side

I think Will Rogers might have been right about life and golf. Rushing through things ends up costing us more time than it saves. In recent years neuroscience has confirmed the fact that learning takes time and rushing through experiences deprives our brain of the time necessary for learning to take place. The brain needs time to change.

Think of a situation where you want to sneak away at lunchtime to the driving range but you only have an hour to practice. Should you hit as many balls as possible (or as many putts, chips, etc.)? Should you take your time, even if it means hitting far fewer balls? Is it even worth the drive to the range? Most people in this situation hurry to the range and without wasting time warming up, they hit balls as fast as possible. They go back to the office frustrated because they weren't hitting the ball very well and on top of that, now their back hurts. Is it any wonder why they didn't seem to have a high quality practice? Here is a simple truth: The number of balls you hit does not equal the amount of learning that happens. Quantity does not equal quality.

Number of balls hit ≠ amount of learning

So, the question again is what if you don't have much time for practice? The best intentioned people generally start their practice at a controlled pace, hitting a ball, taking a little time, hitting another, and so on. But then a curious thing happens. Without realizing it, they speed up. Maybe it is an internal clock that says they should hurry up and get on to the next thing they need to do that day. Maybe they start worrying about a miss-hit a ball and they want to hurry and hit the next ball, trying to get the taste of a bad shot out of their mouth as quickly as possible. They rake another ball to correct the mistake and rather than slowing down or taking a few seconds to regroup, they speed up. The quick reload and re-hit results in another poor shot, and the snowball from hell starts.

> ### *TRAINING TIP FOR THE RANGE*
>
> Next time you go to a driving range near closing, or you go to the course just before a shotgun start tournament, notice what the players are doing. Most players start out at a comfortable pace, but as time progresses their pace quickens. Have you seen it, the rapid fire hitting when there is a last call on the range or a player only has a short time until their tee time? The players get faster and faster trying to hit more and more balls before the final bell tolls. Somehow these players equate quality and quantity. It just ain't so. Those last few balls, those ever so important last few balls that give you the tempo for the first tee, are often hit at a tempo much faster than ideal. Instead, you should hit the last few balls with the tempo you want on the course. Here is a simple solution. Hit a ball and then make yourself watch it until it comes to a complete stop. I'm not talking about watching it until you know where it is going, I mean watch it until it comes to a complete stop. Try it; I think you will be surprised at how it helps your tempo and calmness.

Hitting several balls in rapid succession not only creates a fast tempo, it also deprives the brain of the time necessary to understand and store the information. Time is required for learning.

The passage above is correct in that the learning of skill does in fact cause a physical changes. Specifically, scientists now know that when we learn, our brain changes, it is rewired with the new information. This process of re-wiring takes time. In some cases it may be seconds, in others it may be days. One thing that dictates how quickly practice changes the brain is how much meaning it carries with it. So, the best way to learn requires that you attach meaning and give your brain enough time to process the information.

Focus on quality, not quantity

TWO TYPES OF PRACTICE

Massed practice means that you practice en masse. In other words, you practice more than you rest. Scraping and hitting, scraping and hitting, is an example of massed practice. Since you have read the earlier sections and you are now highly knowledgeable in learning, and you could guess that massed practice is one example of what was called repetitive practice. As we have already discussed with repetitive practice, massed practice may seem like a good idea to the untrained eye, but it is not ingraining the information into memory. This is an example of quantity over quality. Although massed practice is clearly not the

> **For the scientists**
> There is neurological evidence that the acquisition of a motor skill does in fact cause a physical change within the organism, that there does develop some kind of groove– a wiring diagram, a magnetic affinity, a set of internal neurological connections, **something**. Some thing. If this is true (and it is generally assumed to be so, never mind the difficultly in locating or measuring or defining it), if an athlete can encode a skill within his or her body, then there must be room to improve the encoding. In the chinks and gaps among the swarm of factors identified as influencing the acquisition of skill there must be points of access. Exploring those points of access will contribute to the performance revolution to come. *(Adapted from the Sweet Spot in Time)*

best way to practice for most golfers, it is the exact way most golfers practice.

Spaced practice means that you rest more than you practice. In this regard it is the opposite of massed practice. One great example of this is Ben Hogan. I know, if you know anything about Hogan's legendary practice regiment you my think it is the furthest thing from restful practice, but the idea of more rest than practice doesn't mean that you hit a shot and lie down for 10 minutes. It means that you take time to digest each shot and this is exactly what Hogan did. For him each shot had a purpose and a target by thinking of each shot Hogan extended the time between each ball he hit. This is an example of quality over quantity.

For spaced practice, you may hit a shot (or a few shots) and take a short time to think about your swing before you hit more shots. Sometimes this can be done as easily as picking a new target or going through your preshot routine every few shots. Spaced practice is what most players should do because it gives time for elaboration and it simulates what is actually done during a round. Think about it this way; you never hit 10 balls in rapid succession on the course, but many players do exactly that on the range.

> OK, I said you never hit 10 balls in rapid succession on the course but I have seen a player, during a tournament round, hit three balls in less than 30 seconds. At a NCAA regional event the weather had turned bad, so bad in fact that they had to stop play to let the hail on the greens melt. On #10, a long and tight par-4, the wind was blowing hard from left to right. The player, at the time ranked #1 among collegiate golfers, hit a good drive in the fairway. For his second shot, he hit the ball so badly that as it reached the out of bounds line it was still climbing. It was a dead shank. Before the ball had hit the ground he pulled a second ball from his pocket and dropped it on the fairway. The two balls hit the ground in nearly perfect synchrony. The second ball was hit without a practice swing and it too went wide right. A third ball was retrieved from the bag, dropped, and hit in rapid succession. This one found the green.

If spaced practice is better than massed practice, why do most golfers use massed practice?

There are several reasons golfers use massed practice. First, they don't know that massed practice is not an efficient way to learn. Massed practice seems to work, at least during practice time on the range. One of the ironies of massed practice is it can result in good performance during practice. For example, putting the same five foot putt time after time will generally result in making most of the putts. Even though performance is good learning is not. The problem is that the information is not getting deep into the brain. People who use massed practice get frustrated because they do well during practice but don't play any better on the course. They don't know that good practice does not mean good learning.

There might be another reason golfers don't use spaced practice, and you may run into this yourself. Spaced practice is more difficult than massed practice. To do it correctly takes discipline and patience. In short, spaced practice requires effort, but the extra effort pays dividends in the long run. Remember Goldilocks and the Three Bears? Not too easy and not too difficult is where you need to be, so some degree of challenge on the range is good. In fact, most times more challenge than you would want is a good way for range practice. However, most people shy away from more challenge because they don't understand how much it helps or their ego gets in the way. At this point I realize I am being a bit repetitive from earlier chapters, but it is for a reason. A key point in how we learn is that learning comes through challenge. There a several ways to create this challenge but the basic principle holds true. Challenge yourself in practice so you feel less challenged in competition.

Challenge yourself in practice so you feel less challenged in competition

More challenge means a greater likelihood of missed shots, at least in the beginning. Stop thinking of these shots as embarrassing and start thinking of them as learning opportunities. When you can stop fearing bad shots on the range you will take a major step to stopping the fear of bad shots on the course.

When you can stop fearing bad shots on the range you will take a major step to stopping the fear of bad shots on the course

The science behind the effect

Years ago in a laboratory it was discovered that if an individual were given time between trials they learned better, in fact much better. Interestingly enough, the biological principle was originally discovered in experiments with fruit flies. No need to try to imagine fruit flies hitting golf balls; they were learning a simple task (finding food) but this finding gave researchers the idea that it may work for humans as well. Since then, the same idea has been tested on many animals and humans, and time after time it has been found that time between practice trials can help learning. One study published in 1996 suggested that humans need about 24-hours to consolidate the information in the brain. This may be one reason why swing changes take time to set in. However, I don't suggest waiting a day between each shot on the range.

Let's put this idea into some more concrete terms. A couple of years ago my colleagues and I conducted a study examining three groups of golfers. The groups differed in the number of balls they hit during several days of practice. Group A hit as many balls as they wanted during each 90-minute practice session. The other two groups were restricted in the number of balls they were allowed to hit during each 90-minute practice session. Group B hit for approximately 15 minutes, then stopped for about five minutes, hit, stopped, hit, stopped, and so on for each 90-minute practice session. Group C also hit for approximately 15 minutes, then stopped for about 15 minutes, hit, stopped, etc for each 90-minute practice session. All groups practiced for five days at 90 minutes per day. After all the practice was completed, the golfers were tested for accuracy (how close they came to the target on average). As you look at the graph notice that the higher the score the high the accuracy of the shots.

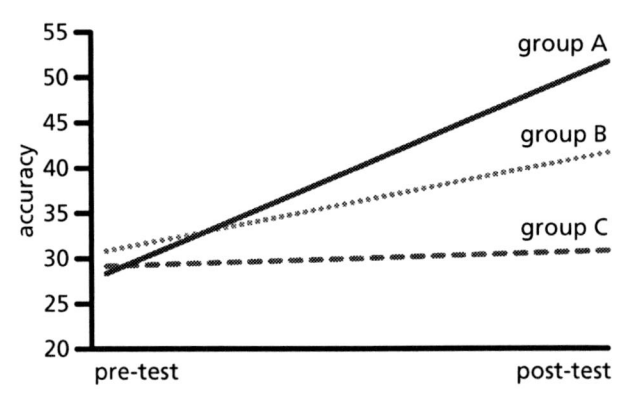

The graph shows that before training starts (pretest) all the groups were equal, but after training (post-test) the group that hit the fewest balls had the best on accuracy on their shots.

Graph reading 101-3: The vertical (y) axis shows performance. In this case, the performance is how well you are doing on the task. Up on the axis means you are increasing the accuracy of your shots and down means you are decreasing shot accuracy. The horizontal (x) axis shows scale. In this case it when the tests occur. The first column is a pretest which shows how accurate each group is before any training. The three groups were equally inaccurate on the pretest. The second column shows the post-test which shows how accurate each group is after training. The three groups did differ on accuracy after training

All the groups started at the same level, but by the end of five days of practice the group that hit the *fewest balls* (spaced practice) *learned the most*. The group that hit the *most balls* (massed practice) *learned the least!* How could this be? How could it be that you can hit fewer balls and learn more? The reason is elaborative and spaced practice.

Group A was left to practice as they chose, and as expected, they chose massed practice. They tried to hit as many balls as possible during the 90-minute session. After all, the balls were free so why not take advantage? As with most people, Group A confused quality and quantity. Since they could hit as many balls as they wanted and were not required to stop and think about anything, they were using repetitive/ massed practice. The other two groups were given time between sets of balls. During this time, they were working on *elaboration*, just like the elaboration discussed in earlier chapters, and they were spacing out the practice. Group B was required to elaborate a little, and Group C, the group that learned the most, was required to elaborate a lot. This isn't to suggest that elaboration is more important than actual physical practice, but it does show that time to think is an important part of practice because it allows time for memories to form and allows time for elaboration.

Too often people are in a hurry when they practice, which is ironic considering that golf is not a hurry up kind of game. Fast practice not only builds bad habits and a quick tempo, it also deprives the brain of the time necessary for learning to take place. Few people elaborate too much during practice but many elaborate too little. The combination between elaboration and allowing the brain time to process information seems to be the most efficient way to practice when you practice without a coach.

SUMMARY

♦ Spaced practice allows time between golf swings. That time allows the structural changes in the brain than need to take place for learning to occur.

♦ Match the spacing to the goal of practice. The more you want to learn from a shot the more you space between shots.

Examples of SPACED practice

Full swing

For the sake of this example, let's say you have an hour to practice full swing. Before you ever get to the range organize practice into sections. Warm up for 5 minutes, take 10 minutes working on tempo by taking a wedge and hitting ½ shots and ¾ shots. This will be difficult to do until you get the right mindset. Most people want to start hitting full shots as quickly as possible. It is exactly this attitude that makes practice inefficient. By practicing tempo for 10 minutes you are accomplishing several important goals. The most obvious of which is that you are working on tempo, but don't underestimate the importance of this. Good tempo can save a lot of bad swings on the course. By working on tempo you are also working on discipline and control. These too are important during a round. Making discipline and control part of your habit will pay off richly during a round. So spend a little extra time working on the finer points by working on tempo.

Good tempo can save a lot of bad swings

After your tempo session step away and remind yourself of the feel of your tempo. Take a little extra time here. When people rush from warm up to hitting they can destroy the good work they just put in. During this time I like to clean my clubs as a way to move slowly. This is your time. Try not to spend it talking with others on the range. If you keep to yourself and feel the tempo and temperament you just created you will find a great calm that will be important for the next section of practice.

The next section of practice will last about 15-minutes, and it is the bubble drill. Make an imaginary circle around your hitting area. You should be able to make a full swing without hitting the sides of the 'bubble.' The game you play here is that no matter what happens outside of the bubble, once you step in nothing and nobody can enter your bubble. Exercise a solid preshot routine including target, posture, practice swings, etc. Hit the shot and watch it until the ball comes to a stop. Then step out of the bubble before you hit your next shot. Work your clubs up and down, hitting three or four shots with each club. If your goal is to engrain a habit, you may hit as many as six different clubs during this time, with no more than three shots per club. If your goal is to discover or start to create a new habit, you will only hit two or three clubs, but you will hit as many as 15 shots with each. The logic behind this approach is the same Challenge Point talked about before. If you don't have a consistent swing you don't want to change too many things at once. That would be too much challenge. Keep the club consistent if your swing is inconsistent. A player with a good habit should change clubs because when the swing is consistent changing the club creates the challenge needed to learn.

Keep the club consistent if your swing is inconsistent and keep the clubs inconsistent if your swing is consistent

The third section of practice will also last 20 minutes. In this section you think through each shot before you hit it. This means that if you are working on something in particular you think through it and visualize it before each swing. For example, if you are working on a particular position at the top of your swing, picture it, feel it, then step into your bubble and execute it. Using this method you are taking the time and putting in the effort to elaborate in a controlled fashion. During this section of spaced practice it will take you somewhere between 30 seconds to a minute to hit each shot. Therefore, in a 20-minute session, you will only hit about 30 balls. I think the first few times you try this you will be surprised how much energy it takes to hit 30 balls. If this is true, it tells you how little effort your old practice was. Remember, effort leads to learning.

Finally, the last section is a 5-minute tempo session. Simply hit tempo shots with any club in your bag. You don't need to go through a preshot routine here. Each time you swing step out of your bubble and them back in for the next swing. This second tempo

> The practice plan just detailed is pretty regimented. You will see shortly that there is room for other types of practice based on what you are trying to accomplish. For example, in what will be called "Discovery" one of the great practice methods is a fun shots drill. During the drill you try to hit sweeping cuts or diving draws. You hit a 6-iron out of a green side bunker or try to hit shots with your eyes closed. But there is a time and place for everything. Right now you need to finish the foundation before you start adding the fine touches to the building.

session is a reminder. Even with control you are still hitting shots more quickly than on the course and so your tempo may have increased. Use this time to remind yourself of the tempo you want.

Putting

Spaced practice for putting is very similar to spaced practice for the full swing. Start by dropping three or four balls on the green and spending 5 minutes with tempo putts. Putt to an area rather than a hole. These putts are similar to lag putts and are designed to let you feel your stroke without being constrained to a target. Most golfers are very goal oriented so if there is a hole they will try to make the putt, and sometimes this can mean that mechanics will be sacrificed for outcome. Removing the hole for the first several putts lets you feel the mechanics before you work on the outcome (making the putt). This creates a much smoother transition to the next set of drills.

During the next 10 minutes practice putting by hitting three putts in a row on the same line to the same hole. Change distance and direction every three putts, but stay within three to five feet of the hole. See how the ball is rolling. See if there are any tendencies like you tend to miss right. Notice the speed of the green. Take your time and pay attention to what is going on.

Spend the next 10 minutes going through your full pre-putt routine. Survey the putt, decide on the speed and line, picture what you are trying to do and then hit the putt. Each putt should take between 30 and 60 seconds this way. The last thing in putting just like the last thing in full swing is tempo. Spend another five minutes with tempo and distance putts. At this point you should be able to really feel what you are doing during the putts.

The putting routine just laid out will only take 30 minutes. Ideally you commit more time than that to putting but 30 minutes of efficient practice will certainly benefit you more than an hour of aimless putting.

NOTE: For putting or full swing you may choose to practice longer. If you are so inclined you can expand the time on each task a little or you can keep the times the same and add a new task. Throughout the following chapters and in the Workbook section there are many other practice methods that you can include.

> ### *Key Points*
>
> ♦ Massed practice means more practice than rest
>
> ♦ Spaced practice means more rest than practice
>
> ♦ Challenge yourself in practice so you feel less challenged in competition
>
> ♦ Good tempo can save a lot of bad swings on the course
>
> ♦ Keep the club consistent if your swing is inconsistent and keep the clubs inconsistent if your swing is consistent

Variety is the Spice of Life

Nobody said that learning had to be complicated. A few simple rules and it works like a charm. Greg Allman and I agree in that we both like variety, but perhaps our reasons are different. My reason is that variety during practice does a lot of good for learning.

Early on I mentioned that elaboration was the way to practice. Elaboration requires that you integrate the information you are trying to learn with what you already know. In other words, elaboration creates a link between the new and the old. This process takes time and it takes creating meaning for what you are trying to learn. In golf the idea of meaning can be as simple as understanding what is correct form. For example, understanding a correct club position at the top of the swing adds meaning. Understanding why it is important to keep your head still on putts adds meaning to what you are trying to learn with putting mechanics. You can also add meaning by using analogies. You may remember that I learned an appropriate correct club position in my golf swing by thinking of a waiter holding a tray. All of this is useful to learning but there is a slight problem with it. All of these examples require you to think during practice. In and of itself thinking during practice is not an issue. However, the problem arises when those thoughts creep onto the course. You cannot be in 'the zone' with a lot of swing thoughts running through your head. The good news is that there is a way to practice that adds meaning without requiring a great deal of thought, at least not in the way we normally think about it. This type of practice, discussed next, is called variable practice.

Constant and Variable Practice

Of the many ways to practice one of the most important comes from an understanding of constant and variable practice. Constant practice is, as the name implies, constantly practicing the same thing. For example, on the practice range it is common to see a person hitting a 7-iron to the same target time after time. Hitting the same club to the same target, or repeatedly putting the same putt is constant practice. You are constantly doing the same thing. By this point I am sure you could guess that that constant practice is usually not a good way to practice.

The opposite of constant practice is variable practice, in which there is a great deal of variety in shots hit during practice. For example, changing clubs and/or targets after each shot creates variety. Likewise, on the putting green changing the distance and direction for each putt you hit is variable practice.

The question of which type of practice is better for you, constant or variable, is partially answered by your expertise level, and what you are trying to learn. Once again, the Challenge Point can shed some light on this idea, but before we talk about that it is important to understand the mechanics of constant and variable practice a little more. To do this, I am going to give you a little math quiz. There are two parts to this quiz. You have 20 seconds for each part. Solve all the equations out loud. After you have solved the equations for Section 1 take a one minute break.

> **SECTION 1**
>
> $52+45 =$
>
> $52+45 =$
>
> $52+45 =$
>
> $52+45 =$

Wait for 60 seconds....now solve section 2 equations in 20 seconds.

SECTION 2

55+36 =

28+45 =

52+45 =

66+35 =

Notice anything? For Section 1 most people only figure out the answer to the first problem and then recognize that it is the same problem over and over again. Then, there is no need to keep figuring out the answer, simply restate the answer rather than figuring it out each time (or just said to you that they are the same). So even though there are four equations, you only figure out the answer once. The reason for this is that humans are by nature very efficient (some would say lazy). If there is no reason to go to the effort of figuring out an answer you already know, you won't go to the effort.

Obviously the equations in Section 2 don't afford you the same easy system. For Section 2, when you figure out the answer to the first equation you are still not done. You need to calculate the second, third, and fourth. Solving the problems in this second set of math problems is more difficult and takes more effort. Also, if you are trying to do it fast, you may make mistakes. As you can see, solving the same problem time after time is much different than solving a different problem each time. In other words, if the problem is constant it is much easier but you are not learning much. If the problem changes each time, or is variable, it is more difficult but you learn more.

Now if we leave it at that, it would be pretty simple to guess that constant practice is easier than variable practice. Constant practice takes less effort, and because of this one typically performs well under constant practice. This is precisely the reason most people use constant practice on the driving range. It is easier and because they are performing well they think they are learning. However, based on the Challenge Point theory, performing well during practice does not make for the best learning. The graph below is very similar to the ones shown in earlier chapters.

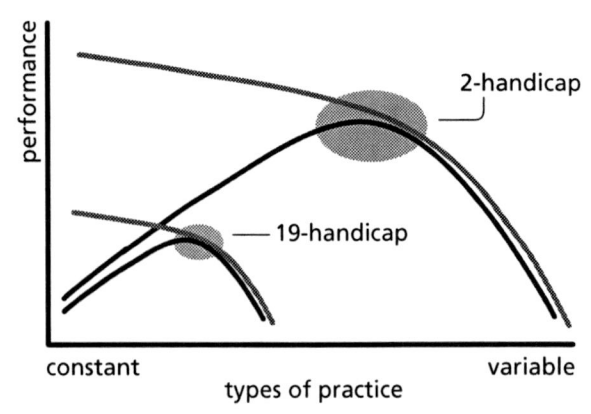

The graph shows constant and variable practice and how they relate to expertise. Constant practice is better suited for inconsistent swings (beginners) where as variable practice is better for consistent swings (experts).

As you have seen several times so far, the same basic curve exists between performance and learning. As the challenge increases performance gets worse but learning gets better (at least to a point). In this example we are changing the challenge by making the practice constant or variable. Constant practice is easier than variable practice because with constant practice you are solving the same problem over and over again. According to Challenge Point, the more expertise you have the more you should engage in variable practice. For the 2-handicapper the optimal challenge point is toward the variable (right) side of the graph. The swing is consistent and so challenge is created by making the club or target inconsistent. However, the same amount of variability would overwhelm the 19-handicapper. Here, the optimal challenge point is more toward the consistent (left) side of the graph. The swing is inconsistent and so the appropriate challenge is created by keeping the club or target consistent. In the case of both the 2-handicapper and the 19-handicapper the basic curve looks the same. Where practice performance is challenging learning is optimized. The only difference is at what point of variability the appropriate challenge comes.

You probably have already picked up a subtle point; constant practice is very similar to repetitive practice. Both forms of practice allow you to perform well during practice because they provide relatively little challenge. However, this same lack of challenge hinders your ability to learn. This is one of the reasons people perform better on the range than they do on the course. Think about it this way; if we are asked to figure out the same problem over and over, we will take the easy way out. All we do is recognize that it is the same problem and give the same answer, just like in the example of the constant math problem. If we get the answer wrong, we simply adjust the answer a little and give the new answer. We don't go through the steps to figure it out again. Humans are efficient by nature, which means that we rarely output energy unless we have to. Unfortunately, it is exactly this output of intellectual energy that is necessary for learning.

In the math example you may have performed well with Section 1 problems but you were not learning anything about the rules of math. The only thing you were learning was to recognize that the problems are the same. However, if the problem is different every time, like in the variable math problems, you have to go through the steps to figure out the answer each and every time. It is slower this way and you may not be as good initially, but you are learning the rules of math. In the long run, taking more time and using intellectual energy to do so is a much more efficient way to learn.

So how does this apply to golf practice? Take putting as an example. If we want to learn to putt better, making the same putt time after time is like solving the same math problem time after time. We may fool ourselves into believing that we are learning how to putt because we are performing well, but we are probably just using repetitive processing. Typically in this scenario, if you leave a putt short you don't recalculate the next putt, you just hit it harder. This is similar to missing a math problem by saying the answer is 96 when the actual answer is 97. Next time you don't recalculate the answer if it is the same question, you just alter what you did last time. Getting the answer right is not the key to learning. Learning how to solve the problem is the key to learning.

Getting the answer right is not the key to learning. Learning how to solve the problem is the key to learning

The good news about all this is that we can take this information and create an efficient learning schedule. As with massed and spaced practice, we will provide examples of full swing and putting.

SUMMARY

Which is better, constant or variable practice? It depends on your level of expertise. The better golfer you are the more variability you should create during practice. This means, the 1-handicaper should switch clubs every few shots (3-5). However, the 20-handicap should have little club variability (12-15 shots) because they already have enough variability to challenge the system without changing clubs.

Examples of VARIABLE practice

You will notice several similarities between the examples you are about to read and those that you read with spaced practice. Spaced practice has a great deal in common with variable practice. Both types of practice impact the degree to which information is elaborated upon. However, they differ in how automatically each creates elaboration. Spaced practice is controlled by time and it allows you to think about the swing and what you are trying to do. Variable practice, on the other hand, creates a situation in which you become an automatic problem solver. By solving several similar problems, such as how to hit golf shots with different clubs, your brain develops an understanding of the rules of the golf swing. Ideally this understanding happens automatically rather than requiring you to think about how to swing the club. This is just like the math example in which you had to figure out the rules of math to solve each different problem, hitting the golf ball with different clubs

If variable practice is automatic why not use it instead of spaced practice? One of the advantages of spaced practice is that it takes time, and this time, in addition to helping you learn, helps to keep your tempo smooth. Spaced practice also simulates the time between shots like the course. Variable practice engages automatic memory but it does so by changing the equation you are trying to solve. However, if, like in the math example, you are not good at the basic rules of math, changing the equation every time creates too much challenge and overwhelms the system. The solution is to use both variable and spaced practice. Use each when appropriate. Early in learning or when you are trying to work on tempo, spaced practice is good. When you are working on consistency and choosing a club for a target, variable practice is best. Finally, combine the two by changing clubs and taking time between shot, but only do this if you are at the final stages of refinement.

lets you understand some general rules about the golf swing including ball position, set up, and the general swing. Variable practice seems to create an ability to "automatically" learn the important variables of the skill.

Variable practice seems to create an ability to "automatically" learn the important variables of the skill

Full swing

Just like spaced practice, it is best to organize practice into sections. For that matter, if all you do is organize practice into sections and set a goal for each practice session you are ahead of the game. Once again, you have an hour to practice full swing. After warm up, take 10 minutes working on tempo by taking a wedge and hitting ½ shots and ¾ shots. You will be amazed at how often you can use this shot on the course. Remember, during this first section you are establishing tempo. Then, step away and think about the tempo, wash your club, and move on to the next section of practice. Establish your bubble just like you did with spaced practice. Take 15 minutes and work your clubs up and down.

For the *high handicapper* this means that you switch between a short iron, mid-iron, and wood, hitting five shots with a club, then stepping away and hitting another five shots. After 10-15 shots switch clubs (the higher the handicap the more balls you hit per club). NOTE: never hit more than five balls in a row without stepping away and thinking about what you have done.

For the *low handicapper* this means that you switch between any club in your bag, hitting three to five shots with a club, then stepping away and hitting another three to five shots. After 9-15 shots switch clubs (the lower the handicap the fewer balls you hit per club). NOTE: never hit more than five balls in a row without stepping away and thinking about what you have done.

As mentioned earlier, the idea here is to keep the club consistent if your swing is inconsistent and keep the clubs inconsistent if your swing is consistent. The third section of practice will last 30 minutes. In this section you play a round of golf. For each virtual hole you play choose clubs just like you would on the course. To do this, you can use a score card from any course you would like. Play Spyglass, St. Andrews, Augusta, or the course you have for your next tournament. Before you go to the range download the scorecard for the course you are going to play. Go through each shot just like you would on the course. That means that you use your preshot routine, consider the shot and the appropriate club you want to hit, then step into the bubble and hit the shot. If you hit a good tee shot, your next shot may require a 9-iron. If you hit a bad tee shot you may need to punch out into the fairway or use a longer iron to the green. Switch clubs each shot just as you would on the course. You may only get to play a few holes practicing this way, but remember, quality is your guide, not quantity. Finally, the last section is a 5 minute tempo session. Simply hit tempo shots with a higher lofted club like 9-iron or wedge. Like always, this tempo session is designed to teach you tempo, so take your time.

Putting

Spaced practice for putting is very similar to spaced practice for the full swing. Start by dropping three or four balls on the green and spending 5 minutes with tempo putts. Remember, tempo putts are to an area rather than a hole. These putts are similar to lag putts and are designed to let you feel your stroke without having the pressure of making a putt. Spend the next 10 minutes hitting one to three putts in a row to a hole. Change distance and direction more often as your skill improves. After 10-minutes of this, play a putting game. Similar to the full swing game, create situations where you have hit an approach shot onto the green and now you have a putt. Play it out just like during your round. Set up long and short putts just like when you play. Spend time with each putt just like you would during a round. Notice your tendencies. If you tend to leave putts short, start hitting putts with more pace. Use this as an opportunity to learn to read greens, decrease negative tendencies, and enhance mechanics. Finally, spend another five minutes with tempo putts.

SUMMARY

All practice is not equal. Anyone who wants to learn should want a better way to practice. The practice schedules just suggested differ from the typical practice in several important ways. Most players, when they hit the same putt, don't go through their routine of lining up the putt, practicing the stroke, etc. It takes too much time and too much discipline. It is easier to just hit the putt, make an adjustment, hit the putt, and so on. The time between putts is only a matter of a few short seconds. However, if you change the putt every time, you take more time because you have to read the putt each time, and you have to go through the process of deciding on pace and line. By having to solve the "putting problem" every time you will learn the rules for good putting. You can do the same thing on the range by hitting shots with a new club to a new target every time. This method will require you to recalculate each shot. The more you recalculate on the range the better you will be when you have to calculate on the course. Recalculating the answer in golf, just like recalculating the answer in math, will create deeper more solid memories of the rules of success. You may find this method is more difficult in the beginning but if you are committed to it you will see it pay off many times in the long run. Like I mentioned before: Pay now or pay later.

One more note on variability.

You need to have a fairly well developed golf ability to take advantage of the automatic processes of elaboration. If you are a beginner you are better off utilizing feedback to improve rather than variability. When you start getting better, move to feedback and spaced practice, and only after you have some basis of the mechanics should you spend most of your time in variability practice. If you try variability too soon it will over challenge the system and this could hurt your chances for learning more than help your chances. If you are in the gray zone and you don't know if you are ready for variable practice, just give it a try. If it seems too difficult or frustrating and the majority of your shots are not good shots, you are not ready. For any practice method, if the majority of your shots are unacceptable, that practice method is unacceptable. Challenge yourself but don't punish yourself.

DOES IT REALLY WORK?

Knowing that elaborative practice works in theory and seeing it in practice are two different things. The role of elaborate and repetitive practice may make sense in the world of science, but does it actually work? Indeed it does. There are many real life examples that show that this works.

One of the best players with whom I have had the pleasure of working was often criticized for not practicing much. It is very true that he would not spend hours upon hours on the range, but this was more the result of efficiency than laziness. When he goes to the range he goes there with a purpose, a goal. He works on one specific thing, intensely but for a short time, and then takes it to the testing ground: the course. By doing this, the quantity of his practice is relatively low, but the quality is very high.

A CASE STUDY OR TWO: VIJAY SINGH

Vijay Singh, the number one ranked player in the world in 2004, has never been criticized for practicing too little. In fact, he is known as one of the hardest workers (if not the hardest worker) on tour. It would be easy to use him as a counter to the idea that quality is more important than quantity. However, if you look closer you will see two interesting points that speak to this issue. First, if you get a chance watch how Vijay works on the driving range. He lays down clubs to work on his alignment, he uses drills to work on aspects of his swing, he hits a variety of shots, and he is constantly elaborating on what he is doing, and Vijay is generally considered one of the very best ball strikers on tour. Second, take a look at how he practices putting. At least in years past he has used a variety of training 'aides' for his putting practice. For example, I've seen him use putting rails for hours on end. It is claimed that the putting rails is a device that guides the putter back and through the ball in a perfect trajectory. The problem is that it guides the putter. Rather than you having to create a putting motion the device guides you. The logic behind such devices is that they are "teaching your muscles" the correct movement. You now know that muscles don't learn (no muscle memory) and so the device is actually guiding performance rather than teaching putting. I strongly suspect that if Vijay changed his putting practice methods he would change his putting statistics. Don't get me wrong, I'm not criticizing Vijay. I would just love to see how good he would be if he used a more efficient way to practice.

So you see, the same work ethic exercised in two different ways yields two different results. Using a great work ethic with elaborative practice yields great results. Using the same work ethic with constant guided practice leaves a lot to be desired, and the problem is compounded if you don't have the time or ability of Vijay Singh.

Key Points

♦ Quality of practice, not quantity, is the key to successful practice.

♦ Take a little extra time and think about what you are doing before, during, and after practice. It will pay off in the long run.

♦ Challenge yourself in practice to help decrease your challenge in competition, but always challenge at the appropriate level.

♦ Concern yourself with how much you are learning, not how good you look on the range.

section three:
Finer Points of Learning

Section I provided you with the mindset that you need to have for efficient learning. **Section II** gave you the tools of learning. In this section we will talk about how to complete the equation. Coordinating your practice goals with the type of practice you choose will increase learning. Finally, we will let neuroscience work for you in the chapter on supercharged learning. Don't skip ahead. Everything is presented in its time.

Discovery, Refinement, and Re-discovery

> My neighbor Val is a genius. He has found a way to keep from falling into one of the classic traps of most golfers. The trap is this: people often feel frustration when their practice does not result in improved golf scores. This is not Val's problem...

REASONS FOR PRACTICE

It may seem obvious that the reason to practice is to learn. For most people this is true, but you can dramatically speed up the process by understanding what you are trying to learn. When I say what you are trying to learn I am not talking about aspects of the golf swing, I am talking about what type of learning you are trying to accomplish. The last section discussed the methods of practice and how to engage the brain in what you are doing. This section goes one step further to streamline the process of great golf by matching your goals of practice to the methods you need to accomplish those goals.

DISCOVER, RE-DISCOVER, OR REFINE

Why do you work? Why do you have a job? Most people, at some level, work to get paid. Would you still work like you do if you knew you wouldn't get paid? Probably not. So why do you practice? For most people the intended payoff for practice is better golf. Have you been practicing golf without the payoff you would like? Granted, practicing golf is generally more fun than going to work, but at the end of the day you still would like to get rewarded for you efforts, be it in the form of money or learning. In fact, one of the great frustrations in golf is that you practice and practice and it does not result in improved scores on the course.

Not long ago I was talking with my neighbor Val about the frustration people often feel when practice does not result in learning. Val told me that he used to have the same problem but a short while back he had solved this dilemma. Before I go on I think it is important to understand that Val is a genius. He comes up with brilliant solutions all the time, and so when he said he solved this problem I was all ears.

Val's solution: don't practice. His logic was staggering in its simplicity. If you don't practice you don't have any expectations of getting better and so you are never disappointed by the same old golf game. Val is kind of a unique guy and based on the fact that you are reading this book I am presuming you don't want to take Val's approach. So instead of giving up on practice, or just working harder, perhaps it is time for you to work smarter.

When practice doesn't work

Most people fail to get what they want out of practice because of *how* they practice rather than *how much* they practice. I know that in the chapter on elaboration it seemed like I was saying that elaboration is the way to go, and this is generally the case. But to get the whole picture you have to match how you practice to why you are practicing, and this is rarely done. For example, sometimes you want to practice in a way that does not lead to learning, just like there may be times when you are willing to work overtime at your job without getting paid for it. Even though this seems completely contrary to what I just mentioned a few pages ago, there is a method to the madness. Rewards don't have to come immediately for them to be rewards. In some cases, the most impactful rewards are not immediate. In this section we are going to tie goals of practice with practice techniques. This will ensure that you get what you want to get out of each practice session.

MATCHING PRACTICE GOALS TO PRACTICE TYPE

Unlike wine and cheese, people rarely match their practice goal to their method of practice. The reason for this is quite simple: Most people don't have detailed practice goals. For most people, the

Think of practice goals and practice methods like wine and cheese. They should be paired appropriately. Pairing a sweet white wine with a stinky blue cheese does a disservice to both, and at the end of the experience you are not satisfied. Think of practice goals and practice methods in the same way and pair them as such.

practice goal is the practice time. How long will I practice today? As we have talked about before, this is because most people equate quantity with quality. The more I practice the better I will get. Goals focus the efforts and matching them to the methods turns the focus into a laser.

As you will see in the next chapter, goals are important for each practice session just like goals are important for your golf game. However, goals for practice are immediate. That is, you set a goal for a practice session and work on it immediately. Practice goals are a one shot deal and when practice is over, you are done with that goal until the next time you practice. Don't get me wrong here. Practice goals are immediate but they are set up for long term rewards. They are set up not to make you look good during practice but to help you play better on the course. Like we talked about earlier, if you look too good during practice you probably are not challenging yourself hard enough. Practice goals are about practice organization. They are not about instant gratification.

A note on instant gratification

Clearly the attempt to overcome instant gratification is not a golf only problem. Not by a long shot. It happens many many times a day for each of us. In fact, one of the differences between someone who is routinely successful and those who are not is the ability to put aside instant gratification for long term payoffs. We talked about this in the Pay now or Pay later section. One of the best ways to do something for the future is to know the future. It is like a little kid trying to earn enough money to buy a bike. When he makes $5 what is he going to do with it? If he knows that spending it on candy will take him away from his goal he will be less likely to spend it on instant gratification. The same goes for you. If you have a clear goal, a clear outcome in mind, it is significantly easier to make decisions now that will serve that goal rather than making decisions for instant gratification. This is one reason why goals are so vital to success which in turn is one reason why the next chapter is all about goals.

Just like any other goal, practice goals help direct your effort. To set these practice goals, think of practice goals in three categories; *discovery, rediscovery,* and *refinement.*

Discovery, Rediscovery, and Refinement

At one end of the practice spectrum is the goal of **Discovery**, the act of trying to discover something that will help you play better. This is a never ending pursuit for most golfers. In discovery mode you may tinker with your swing, your stance, or your posture trying to discover what works. You are not so interested in refining the skill as you are in finding that skill. At the other end of the spectrum is **Refinement**. This is when you have already discovered what you want in your swing and you are trying to make that your habit. The final goal of practice is right in the middle of discovery and refinement. This final goal is called **Rediscovery,** and it is when you had 'it' at some point, then you lost it, and now you are trying to find it again. For non-golfers, the last sentence may make no sense, but most golfers know exactly what I am talking about. Time after time it seems that we have figured something out that lets us hit the ball better or make more putts, but as soon as it appears it seems to disappear. Rediscovery is about finding that special something again.

Each goal of practice brings with it specific methods of practice that work well and those that do not. Knowing ahead of time what you are trying to accomplish and knowing how to go about it will make practice much more efficient and make play much more rewarding.

Principles like elaborative practice still hold true, but applying them to the appropriate practice goal really speeds things up. That is, there are specific ways to accomplish each goal of practice. If you use the wrong method you are not doing yourself any favors. It's like trying to use a screwdriver to hammer in a nail. There is nothing wrong with the screwdriver per se; it's just the wrong tool for the job. You need the right tool if you want it done correctly. Don't use discovery tools for refining skills, use discovery tools for discovery. The next section will talk about the tools to use for each goal and specific examples of how you can match the goal with the type of practice.

Discovery is like a treasure hunt. You are looking for the po t of gold known as great golf

Discovery is generally helped along by an extra pair of eyes. For example, if you are trying to change your swing plane, it is helpful to have a coach or video camera with you. A teaching professional will know what to look for and how to help you understand the important aspects of the game. By using a teaching professional it is like having a tour guide on the treasure hunt. You have someone discover for you and then teach you what you need to discover. It becomes an efficient model because having someone do the discovery work for you frees up your time to work on refinement (which is eventually where you want to be). This is particularly the case for golfers who do not have an intimate knowledge of the golf swing. If you have a pretty good idea of the golf swing a video can help you discover the swing for yourself. It is also a good record for rediscovery later on. Of course the best of both worlds is to have a video of your lessons.

> Having a teacher with you also provides a refined sense of feedback for you. As discussed earlier, accurate feedback makes for efficient learning.

> When you work with a teaching professional or coach ask them to diagnose the cause, not the effect. Think of this like trying to fix a house. A crack in the ceiling of the house is not the cause, it is the effect. The cause of the problem generally starts from the foundation and until you fix the foundation the effects will keep cropping up. For example, if you pull the ball left you may think that the cause is that you tend to come over the top in your golf swing. In fact, the cause may be your set up and the first effect is the over the top move, and the second effect is the ball going left. Until you fix the set up the cracks will continue.

If you are not working with a teaching pro, then you will need to set up your discovery practice in the repetitive mode. That is, use massed or constant practice. The reason for this is twofold. First, repetitive practice is not for learning the golf swing, but it can be used for discovering a problem or solution. If you are trying several different take away paths, postures, grips, etc, you don't want to learn them all. You only want to learn the one that works. Discovery is about experimentation, and this is partially why you want constant practice.

Any good scientist knows that you should only manipulate one variable at a time. For golf, this means that if you are changing your set up that is all you want to change until you get that figured out. If you try to change both your set up and grip while at the same time alternating clubs, you have too many moving parts. Make the puzzle as simple as possible rather than complicate it by adding layers.

Make the puzzle as simple as possible rather than complicate it by adding layers

CONSIDER: When you use constant or massed practice there is a tendency to speed up tempo. Put a couple of tempo drills in every few minutes when you are in the discovery mode.

When you are trying to discover a feel or position in your golf swing or stance it may help to occasionally take away a source of information. In this case, take away the eyes. This may sound contradictory since we just said that an extra set of eyes is helpful and now I am suggestion to close your eyes, but these two things actually work together. If you close your eyes and feel the position (sometimes you will need someone to put you in the right position to feel it), you can retrain your feel for the position you are trying to achieve. This is very similar to the idea of retraining proprioception talked about in chapter 7.

REMINDER: Proprioception is feedback telling you the positions of your limbs. It tells you where your hands are during the swing.

Retraining your feedback doesn't happen immediately, but over time you will find yourself moving into the right position automatically. Close your eyes, get in position, and then open your eyes and check your position. It helps to have a mirror for this. However, even if you are on the range you can do this but just holding a position and opening your eyes. Also, you can do this with the actual swing. By keeping your eyes closed you will be able to feel the swing better than you can with you eyes open. Be very careful with this drill. If your swing or balance are off you will know in a hurry. Try it in slow motion at first and gradually speed up as you are ready. You can also use the same drill for putting.

The advantage of taking away vision is based on the idea that vision is such a powerful sense. If you have your eyes open vision will drown out the other senses. On the other hand, if you close your eyes you will become more keenly aware of your other senses including your body positions (proprioception). You have probably heard stories of the blind man who has very good hearing. The idea is that if one sense is taken away the others become keener.

Closing your eyes allows you to better focus on your positions and retrain your limbs for the proper position

One last note: even if you have a coach at your disposal, I would encourage you to work by yourself some of the time. If you are the one who discovers something that works you are more likely to remember it than if someone just tells you what to do. It is the old idea *"If you give a man a fish he eats for a day. If you teach him to fish he eats for a lifetime."* This same logic holds true for some training aides. Many of them are designed to guide you to a position. This is not bad in and of itself, but if you come to rely on a training aid to put you in the right position or move in the correct path you will not be learning how to create that path or position. You will simply learn to use the training aid. For you to learn how to do something you have to do something. With this in mind, use training aids in moderation and for the best results use each method (training aides, a coach, no vision) on occasion but not habitually.

For you to learn how to do something you have to do something

THREE RULES TO DISCOVERY

Rule 1: Only manipulate one variable at a time. This means that rather than changing the grip, stance, and posture all at once, change one at a time to see what happens. If you change your grip and stance and your swing is different, you don't know whether it was grip, stance, or both that made the change.

Rule 2: Simple first. This rule is commonly referred to as Occam's razor, which states that a problem should be stated in its basic and simplest terms. In golf, this means simple first. Before you start thinking of lots of complicated fixes to your swing, think simple. Ask yourself, "What is the simplest thing I can think of to improve my swing?" Many times, it is something very simple. Check you posture, focus on finishing the swing, focus on a slow take-away, etc. Don't get complicated unless simple doesn't work, but simple almost always works.

GAPS. Scott Cowan, a very good friend and great teacher once said that "90% of all the lessons I give address GAPS: grip, alignment posture and stance, as the major cause of a swing error." Mike Moore adds balance to this equation. Regardless of your list, go to the basics first before you try to complicate things.

Rule 3: Use repetitive and constant practice. This way you keep the variables the same and because the practice is repetitive, you are less likely to learn swings you don't want to learn. Later you can change the type of practice to refine the skills.

What you should and should not expect in the discovery mode

When you are in a discovery mode, don't expect to hit the ball well all the time. In fact, for most people the reason they find themselves in the discovery mode is because they are not hitting the ball well. If you are already playing great you will spend most of your time in the refinement mode not the discovery mode. In the discovery mode your goal is to find the swing, not groove it. To do this you need to experiment with different swing thoughts and mechanics. Some of these experiments are going to work better than others. Don't concern yourself with the bad shots you hit on the way to discovery. You want some failures so you know what doesn't work. Remember, you are disrupting what you are doing to find a better way. In fact, in a study we published just a couple of years ago we found that the more the swing is initially disrupted (during the discovery mode) the more improvement takes place in the long run. It never feels good to hit the ball badly, but know that when you are disrupting the swing in the short term you are improving it for the long term. Buy into the process and discover your best swing, even if it means hitting a few bad shots along the way. You are in this for the long run, not just for one day on the range.

One final note on discovery. Remember to keep a good tempo. A lot of time the tempo gets faster and faster with each shot. This can wreak havoc on your golf swing. Just because you are in the discovery mode doesn't mean that you can forget your basics. Keep a good pace by stepping away from the pile of balls after each shot or watching a shot until it finishes. Use the 5-ball rule (hit 5 balls and step away) and regain your tempo when you step away.

> ### What If game
> A very fun game I like to play in the discovery mode is the What If game. The rules are pretty simple. All you do is try all kinds of shots. Before a shot ask yourself, "What if I..." What if I opened the club face as far as it will go? How high can I make the ball go? What if I close my stance and hood my clubface? What if I move the ball position way back in my stance? Try a lot of different things just to see what happens. Then, just note what happened. Don't judge it as good or bad, just pay attention to what it is. It is a great way to experiment with Discovery and you never know when one of these shots may come in handy.

An example of DISCOVERY without a coach

First and foremost you need to have the right mindset for discovery. You need to go to the range with the idea that you are on a quest. Think about what you are trying to accomplish before you start. Plan on hitting a few bad shots as you push the envelope and be happy when you do. This will allow you to find your way to the golf swing you want. This is one of the reasons why games like *What If* are so good. They make it fun to see what happens rather than worrying about hitting bad shots. While you are in discovery refuse to give up on the discovery quest and refuse to allow others on the range to affect you. Don't worry about a few bad shots. Consider each a stepping stone on the journey to success. You would rather have a few bad shots on the range now than on the course later. Believe me, you wouldn't be the first player to sh__k a ball while trying to learn a new swing. It is all part of the process to golf excellence.

After your warm up and tempo drill, start the discovery process by eliminating variables. After the set up, the two most important variables in the golf swing (or putting) are alignment and ball position. There are several ways to do this. In fact, there are training aids designed especially for alignment and ball position. Basically, they are a lot like a carpenter's L. Two lines perpendicular to each other with one aimed down the target line and the other for ball position.

If you don't want to buy one of the training aids you can use your clubs instead. Position the target club parallel to the target and set a second club perpendicular to the target club. The target club will help you aim toward the target and the second club will give you a frame of reference for ball position. This way, you will not have to concern yourself with

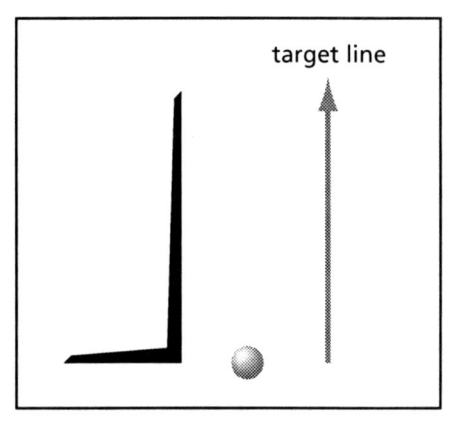

aim and ball position, and you can work on the other aspects of the golf swing.

Choose three clubs that will help with the discovery process. I like a short iron (9-iron), medium iron (6-iron) and a wood (3-wood). This way you can see if your swing tendencies are consistent across clubs. If you have a video camera, film three swings with each club with a ball and without a ball. You are looking for consistency. Do you have a similar swing with each club? Do you have a similar swing with and without the ball? The first part of discovery is finding out what you do. These initial videos help establishing a baseline. The second part of discovery is finding out what you want to do and how to do it.

For the second part of discovery, hit a few balls (e.g., 5) with a single club. I generally start with the short iron. You don't need to go through your preshot routine here because you are not practicing to learn, you are practicing to discover. The preshot will slow you down and make you think. You don't want that right now, at least not much. As such, the discovery practice mode is repetitive or constant practice. Try to understand what needs to change rather than trying to actually make the change. The idea here is that you need to understand what you need before you can get it. Again, if you have a coach they can help you, but if you don't have someone with you discover by paying a lot of attention to what happens. Think a little, but not a lot. Decide what you are trying to do different with your swing. Are you taking the club too much inside? Is your swing too long? Is your setup correct?

REMEMBER: In discovery start simple with GAPS

Determine what you are trying to change and work on that. Work on one thing at a time. Eventually, you will hit the ball the way you like. Now it is time to slow down. Think about what allowed you to hit the ball well and for the next few shots try to replicate that swing. Don't change to the next club until you understand how to make the good swing. Don't feel that you need to hit the ball perfectly every time. Just try to hit it better and be aware of what caused it. Videotape the good swing, then write down what made the difference and give yourself a reminder phrase to help you remember. Reminder phrases such as "low and slow" or "down the line" give a good visual of what you are trying to do. Write it down. I can't overstate the importance of this. Do not trust what you did to memory. If you are like most people you think you will remember but chances are you will not. Writing it down not only gives you a record that you can look back to, the act of writing it down also helps preserve the memory. This is not only true of golf, it is true of every day things. Writing a grocery list will help you remember what you went to the grocery store for. It is the same way with golf. Write it down to remember it.

Write it down to remember it

Once you have an idea of the swing try it out with your mid-iron. If you can't quite get it with your mid-iron, switch back to the short iron until you feel the swing again, then back to the mid-iron. Switch back and forth every few swings until you make the transition to the higher iron. Once you understand the swing with the higher iron, switch to the 3-wood. Again, feel free to switch between clubs if you need to, including going all the way back to the short iron if necessary. Always finish your session with tempo work, but for this second tempo session incorporate the swing change with your tempo drills.

The process of discovery can be a little frustrating if you are on your own. You can decrease the frustration a great deal by keeping a good tempo throughout and allowing yourself to make mistakes. Don't get upset if you hit a few bad shots. You have to push the envelope if you are willing to change.

REMEMBER: You have to let go of good if you want great.

It is better to get a little frustrated on the range than a lot frustrated on the course. On the other hand, sometimes discovery happens early on in a practice session. If this is the case allow yourself to switch to refinement during a practice session.

Refinement is the act of engraining your GAPS, swing, stroke, preshot routine, or anything else you are working on. It is used when you have discovered something that works and you are tying to make it your habit. Many of the practice techniques we have talked about so far help with refinement. Spaced practice, elaboration, variable practice, and feedback all serve to develop new habits. In essence, they all help to establish a new equilibrium point.

Equilibrium is a state of balance. An equilibrium point is that point where everything is in balance. We all have equilibrium points in our everyday life. They are the points where we are most comfortable, and because it is our most comfortable state it is the state we go back to under pressure. Therefore, establishing a good equilibrium point is crucial to performing under pressure. For simplicity sake, an equilibrium point can be considered a habit.

Take the everyday example of walking. Have you ever thought about the reason why you walk at the pace you do? Generally people walk at the speed they do because it is the most comfortable pace. To walk faster or walk slower would take additional mental and physical energy, and that would be less comfortable. In fact, if you have ever walked with someone who walks a lot faster or slower than you do it can be quite annoying. But what if, for some reason, you wanted to make a slower walk your new habit. How do you do it? You need to create a new habit (reset your equilibrium point). It's the same with a golf swing. Each of us has a tendency to take the club back from the ball at a certain pace. That is your habitual pace, and under periods of stress that pace will be most prevalent. If you want to slow your takeaway, you have to reset your habitual pace to a slower rate. Unfortunately, you can't just flip a switch to reset your habit. Instead, you generally have to go to the other extreme and tune the system to move in the appropriate direction. In the walking example, if you want to walk a *little* slower, you would need to walk a *lot* slower, at least for a while. To reset a habit takes time, and in the beginning, it takes effort. In fact, changing any habit takes time and effort, especially in the beginning.

I often think of the idea of changing habits as a rocket going on a mission. The rocket will expend about 80% of its fuel in the first 10% of the mission. Once it has created enough momentum it needs very little fuel to keep going. New habits are the same way. They need a lot of energy to get going but once they have sufficient emotion they continue on the new path with little effort.

So if you currently walk at a rate of 8 (on a scale of 1-10 with 10 being the fastest) and you want to walk at a rate of 5, you need to walk at a rate of 3 or 4 for a while. You will burn a lot of fuel for the first couple of weeks until you have created momentum, but soon what seemed difficult will become easy. It is the same way with a swing change. At first, the change may feel unnatural and you will have to think about it. It is a bad idea to play during this time. Your frustration with results may cause you to revert back to your old ways and will undermine the change you are trying to make. A little patience during the lift off is very well rewarded later in the mission.

After a short while you will notice that parts of the new swing will start to come by more easily, while other parts are a bit less cooperative. As you move closer and closer to changing your habit, it will take less and less effort. Finally the new swing will become your habit and you will need to think of it very little. When this happens you have completed your mission and created a new equilibrium point.

Be patient during the refinement stage. You are asking your brain and body to change and this may take some time. Rushing the job will only delay the result you are looking for. Don't be afraid to practice in front of a mirror or in your garage without hitting a ball. Starting to hit balls too early may cause you to put too much emphasis on the results and not enough emphasis on the process. Ideally, you would like a good part of the swing changes to be automatic before you attempt them on the course. In other words, make sure the process is sound before you focus on the results.

Make sure the process is sound before you focus on the results

One more way to think of this habit or equilibrium point is through a concept called "attractor states." An attractor state means that there is a state, or level, to which we are naturally attracted. In this sense, it is like an equilibrium point.

Take a look at the graph. It is a series of crests and troughs. As you can imagine, the "ball" is attracted to the bottom of the trough. That is, if the ball is anywhere along the curve and it is let go to move where it wants, it will move to the bottom of the trough. This is simply a matter of Physics, but the idea can be extended to the learning of a motor skill.

The graph below shows a series of crests and troughs. The ball at the bottom of trough A represents were you are now and to change the ball needs to move to trough B. This movement requires time and energy.

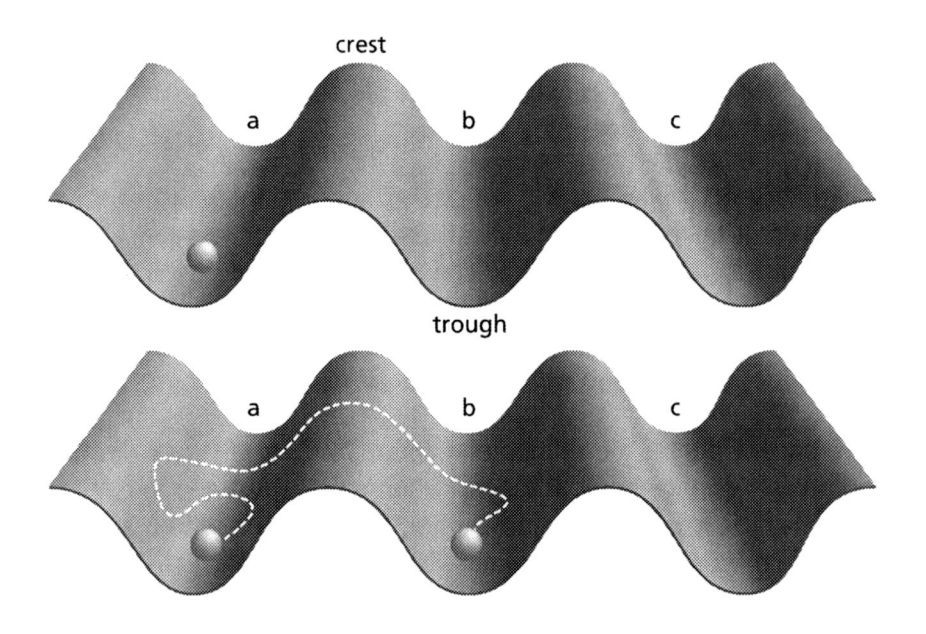

Let's say that your habit (equilibrium point) is the ball at the bottom of trough A, but you want to move your habit point to trough B. For example, you may want to learn a new swing change. Let's say that you have a tendency to come too far inside on your take away so the change you want to make is to take the club more down the line. In the graph, the "new swing" would be trough B. The more you are settled in A, the tougher it will be to get to trough B. Remember, trough A is your old swing. So if you have had your old swing for many years it is going to be difficult, but not impossible to change. As you disrupt your old swing to learn the new swing, you are moving the ball at the bottom of A to B. The closer you are to settling in B, the closer you are to your new swing. Unfortunately, you don't just go from A to B, you have to work your way there. Look at what happens to the ball in the bottom panel as it moves from trough A to B.   First the ball moves toward B, and in this case you seem to making advances to your new swing. This may be during a lesson. Then, a little while later, you actually get worse for a while (moves toward A). With efficient practice and an eye on the process, you can move all the way to B; the new take away you have been trying to achieve. You have now reset your habit so that the new swing is now your comfortable swing. You may experience a phenomenon that I often experience when I am trying to learn a new swing or grip. I remember the new one but I can't remember what I was doing before.

There are three points to make here:

1. Don't be surprised if you take a step back before you take a leap forward. This is just like what happens in the story of good to great.

2. You are not going to be stable until you are in a trough (equilibrium point)

3. If you are not stable you can falter under pressure.

One more note on the idea of equilibrium. Not all crests and troughs are the same. You may have experienced this yourself. Some things are easy to learn and some are not. The easy ones have a small crest and the difficult ones have a large crest. The picture below illustrates how this might look with the attractor states.

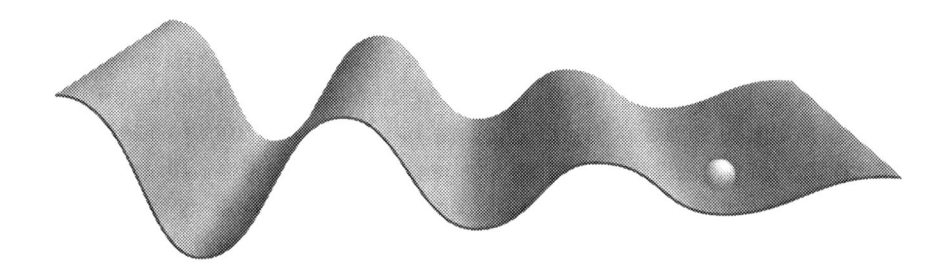

An example of REFINEMENT without a coach

As you might have guessed, the mindsets for discovery and refinement are quite different because the intention of each is quite different. During discovery you are trying to understand what you want to do with a golf swing. During refinement you learn how to make that swing repeatable and automatic. Discovery requires you to push the envelope to understand the golf swing. As such, discovery requires experimentation. On the other hand, refinement is enhanced when you practice in a way to make the new swing become your habit. If you consider that the intentions of discovery and refinement are different, it makes sense that the best way to practice for discovery is not the best way to practice for refinement. Discovery is mostly repetitive practice whereas refinement is mostly elaborative practice. The word "mostly" is very important here. There will be a time during discovery when elaborative practice is best. This is the time when you are transitioning between discovery and refinement. There is also a time during refinement when repetitive practice is best. This is the time you are trying to groove the swing. With this in mind, let's get started with the example.

Even before you go to the driving range, refinement can start. Remember, during refinement you want to make your new swing become your habit. Typically, at the early stages of refinement you have a swing thought to help you with the new swing. For example, you may be trying to learn to start the club down the line rather than immediately bringing it inside. This is the part you need to work on first, but before you can work on it you need to understand what this looks like and feels like. Again, if you have a coach he can show you what it looks and feels like by taking you through that move. I would also recommend that if you have a coach have him video you doing the move correctly so you can refer to it any time you want. Even without a coach you can do this for yourself. Video the move done correctly and watch it so you know what it looks like. At first you may need to exaggerate the move because you have to retrain your senses. If your habitual move is inside and the habit you are trying to learn is down the line, it will initially feel like you are moving the club outside. Remember, our senses can fool us but the video will tell us the truth. For most people the best way to accomplish this initial part of creating a new habit is to do it with a ¾ swing and without a ball.

Simply practice the initial move until it becomes more automatic. Spaced practice works well here. One way to do this is to keep a club in your bedroom or your office. Every time you enter the room or every time you take a break from what you are doing, practice the move five or six times, and remember to pay attention each time. Pure repetition is not going to help as much as if you think about what you are doing. By the end of the day you may have had 30-40 trials of spaced practice.

> It is amazing how frequently the ball gets in the way of the golf swing. I've seen many a golfer with a great practice swing, only to step up to the ball and completely change the swing when the ball is there. Video yourself with and without the ball and see if your swing changes. If it does there are a few drills you can use. First, rather than hitting a ball, hit a tee. This will get you used to hitting something. Once you can do this and your practice and actual swing look alike, hit the ball off a tee until this looks like your practice swing.

Once the new move has started to become your habit, take it to the range. As always, go through your warm up and tempo drill at the start of the session. Remember to set down a club to help with aim and ball position. This way, all your energy can be directed at the task at hand, honing the new move. Take a few minutes to work on the new habit using a ¾ swing speed. Depending how well you have engrained the new move, you might want to get the feel of it without the ball a few times as well. Just work on the part of the swing or set up that you are trying to change. This should take about five minutes. It may be tempting to try the new habit with your driver but resist the temptation. Use a short club like a wedge until you have a pretty good idea of what you are trying to do. This too should take five minutes.

> When people skip the first step of developing a foundation off the course, they are heading for frustration on the course. Without a solid foundation frustration can set in if you go to the course and the new move doesn't work right away. This frustration can cause you to abandon what you are trying to learn for your old way of doing things. If you take a little extra time you will get the payoff down a short road. Otherwise you are in for a frustrating and bumpy ride.

If you are like most people, the ten minutes you spend in these drills will be difficult, but they are necessary.

If you want to be like ordinary people act like ordinary people, and get frustrated like ordinary people. If you want the rapid improvement extra-ordinary people get, then don't behave like ordinary people. The more extraordinary your discipline in the early stages the more extraordinary your progress.

The more extraordinary your discipline in the early stages the more extraordinary your progress.

The discipline needed for success is really just a matter of mindset. If you allow yourself to embrace any struggle that comes your way, little discipline is necessary. This is true in golf and in life. Use the mindset before you get to the practice range and then the 10 minute drill with the wedge will be a joy rather than a burden.

Again with your wedge, hit 3-5 balls with your focus being on the new habit, and evaluate what happens. How would you score your success with the new habit? Did you start the ball down the line? You can use video here as well to evaluate your success. What happened to the ball? Did you hit is well? Make the evaluation and make any corrections you need, then hit another 8-10 balls and go through the process again. Don't change clubs until you have had some success with the wedge, and never hit more than 10 balls in a row. Every time you hit a shot step away from your spot before raking another ball. Take at least a few seconds to think between shots. These few seconds now will allow the habit to become automatic later. Ironically, thinking about the move now will keep you from having to think about it later (on the course). On the other hand, hitting and scraping without thought is using repetitive practice and it will only frustrate you in the long run.

As your new habit becomes more and more automatic, you can move from spaced practice to variable practice. When you have gotten to the point where you can execute the move with only a little thought, change your practice so that you alternate between variable practice and constant practice. For variable practice you will change clubs every few shots, go through your routine of picking a target, set up, posture, and swing. The frequency of changing clubs depends on how automatic your habit has become. The more automatic the more often you switch clubs. For constant practice you hit 5-7 shots in a row with the same club and no preshot routine. It may sound contradictory for me to suggest constant practice here because you know that constant practice can be repetitive practice, and that means no learning. However, there is a reason constant practice works here. At this point, your new habit should be fairly automatic, at least from a mechanical standpoint. By practicing constant practice (the same club several times in a row) you are learning the tempo of the new habit. Additionally, because you understand the golf swing better, it doesn't take much time for your brain to fine tune the new habit and engrain it in memory.

Always finish your practice with tempo drills.

MENTAL VERSUS PHYSICAL EQUILIBRIUM

The equilibrium idea discussed above happens with any change. However, sometimes mental changes and physical changes result in slightly different ways to find their equilibrium points. For example, mental changes can happen exactly as stated above; if you want to change a little, you need to have a big change and then settle back to an equilibrium point. That is, to make something your new habit you sometimes have to go to extremes. This is called a paradigm shift. You need to shift your way of thinking about what you are doing. You need to think differently about it and it needs to be a lot different. If you decide to just think a little differently it will be too easy to slip back. One of my favorite quotes is by Gandhi and says, "Be the change you want to see in the world." For most of us, that requires a paradigm shift. That requires a very different way of thinking and behaving than what is currently happening in the world. Gandhi didn't say "Be a little like the changes you want to see." He knew that to do it you needed to restructure the way you think. In simplest terms, if you don't make it clear to your mind that you are changing you will forget to change. This goes for your attitude on the course as well. If you want to make a change in the way you think make it clear and decisive, and sometimes this means to go to extremes. As shown in the graph the changes take a lot of energy initially to get over the hump.

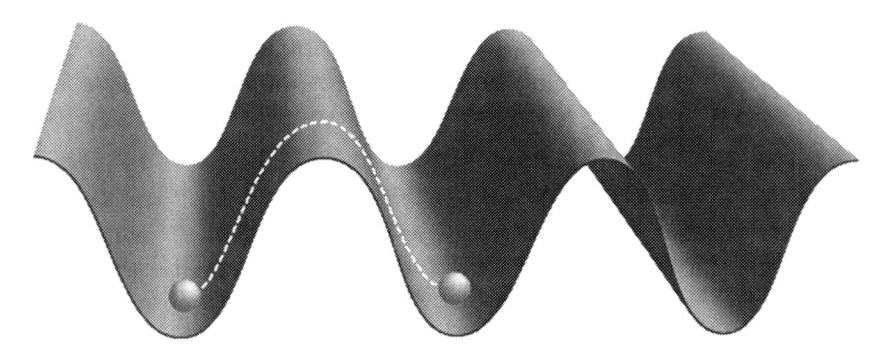

I am not saying that all mindset changes require extreme means, but it is not uncommon to need a life changing event to change your life and mindset. This is not the case with physical changes, and especially with golf. For physical changes you should expect small adjustments until you creep up on the new habit. The reason for this is that making extreme physical changes can result in injury and a lot of frustration. For example, a grip change may seem simple but it can also affect a lot of other aspects of the swing. Let's say that you want to change from a very weak to a very strong grip. To hit a shot with such a dramatic change will also require you to change many other things about your golf swing. That is a lot of moving parts that need to be coordinated, and if the moving parts are not all moving in the same direction something is going to give. This is one of the reasons people get sore after a golf lesson. They are using their body differently than they had been using it.   A good golf teacher will only make minor changes during each lesson. Ironically, this is one reason people often lose patience with physical changes. If they are done correctly they are slow in coming at first. Remember, it took Tiger 18 months to rework his swing. He was patient and disciplined enough to make small physical changes that when added up resulted in a large change.

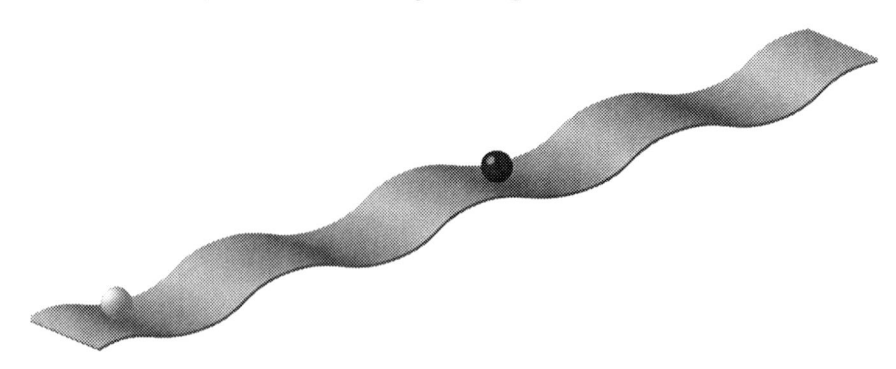

- Mental Changes = extreme crests and troughs

- Physical Changes = small crests and troughs when added together make a large change

An example from the tour

Watching one of my players at a PGA event it seemed he was uncomfortable with nearly every shot. He did a nice job going through his routines and staying focused, and he managed a good first round score largely due to his scrambling ability, but it was an energy expending grind. After the round we talked a bit about what was going on. He felt that he had a good swing but the ball wasn't going where he wanted it to. We went to the range to see what had caused the problem. The first thing checked were the GAPS (grip, alignment, posture, and stance). When you are having a problem with your swing or putting stroke always check the foundation first, because if the foundation is not good, there is little chance that the rest of the swing will be good. Grip, posture, and stance were good. The problem came in the alignment. He was pointed about 10-degrees right of the target. In other words, he had a great set up but it was to the wrong target. His body was set up to one target and his mind was set up to another. This caused the two to be in conflict. Ironically, even though he was aimed right of the target, the ball was going left of the target. His body lined up too far right (closed) and his brain realized this. To get the ball to the target he needed to pull the ball, but sometimes the pull was too extreme and the ball ended up going left.

To correct this conflict the player laid down a target club to ensure proper alignment. As you can imagine, this new alignment felt too far left because he had been training his senses (propriocepton) that right of the target was on the target. Now on the target felt left of the target. After a few balls he began to trust the target club and the alignment and swing came back and he hit the ball well. This continued the next day as he laid down a target club in warm up and played well that day.

This may seem like the end of the story but it is not. Remember, physical changes take time and if you are too aggressive you can over correct. Over the next few days of the tournament the player kept working on his alignment and in fact became so confident that after the tournament he no longer used a target club in practice. By the time I saw him two weeks later he had overcompensated and was slightly open to the target. He had indeed overcompensated.

If you are too aggressive with physical changes it can cause yet another problem.

Fortunately, this time only a slight adjustment had to be made. This process of honing in on the appropriate equilibrium point is quite delicate and nearly always requires an extra set of eyes and/or some type of guidance system like a target club. Just like with any type of guidance, eventually you need to work your way off of it. I say work you way because you get off of the guidance as you have earned it by performing better with out it.

Summary

No doubt you notice the obvious difference between the mental and physical curves. Physical changes need small nudges rather than a single big push. You may have experienced this if you have ever had someone look at your alignment. Once your alignment is corrected it doesn't take a huge effort to use the corrected alignment, you just do it. On the other hand, mental states/attitudes are difficult to change without a concerted effort on your part. The mental curve takes a big push to get over the hump. The good news is that once you get over the hump things settle in pretty well with the new mindset.

The second section of this book is devoted to learning and you may think this is all about the learning of physical skills, but it is not. The ideas from the beginning of the book, such as the zone mindset and can-do attitude can be learned just like physical skills can be learned. The difference between learning the physical and mental skills is the extremes you need to go to. Physical skills change by small steps. Mental changes can be large leaps. Physical changes are generally developed on the range or on the course. It is rare that mental changes are developed on the course. Mental changes are generally developed away from the range and off the course. Then, they are tested on the course. Physical changes generally respond well to feedback, spacing, and variability of practice. Mental changes need feedback, but rather than spacing and variability, you need to be tenacious and consistent for the changes to take root. For mental changes you cannot only practice them sometimes and expect a change.

One final note on this: many times in golf mental changes affect physical changes and physical changes affect mental changes.   For example, if you are worried about hitting the ball in the water (mental) it will generally increase your tension level. An increased tension level can then change your golf swing (physical). On the other hand, if you are confident that you will hit the ball well you are probably at an appropriate tension level and your golf swing is free to flow. Therefore, when you work on your game, remember that to achieve your best golf you need to condition your mental abilities as well as your physical abilities.

One important note about mental and physical abilities.

In the passage above mental abilities and physical abilities were dealt with separately. This was done simply as a means of clarity. In truth, mental and physical abilities are intimately linked. This has been known for thousands of years and at least dates back to the ancient Greek saying, "Mens sanus en coprum sano," which translates to "a sound mind and a sound body."

A great example of mind and body is tension and attention. Tension results from anxiety, fight-or-flight responses, stress, or a variety of sources that cause muscles to increase their rigidity. Tension can make the best swing mechanics poor. Attention is the ability to attend or think about what you are supposed to think about. In golf, you are supposed to think about the present. 'Stay in the present' is one of the key mantras in the game of golf. That means that you think about the shot at hand. That means you do not think about what happens if you miss the shot (future) or the shot you hit two holes ago (past). Although it may seem that tension is physical and attention is mental, they are indeed very closely related. Not realizing the relationship can be the cause of confusion when diagnosing a problem.

Consider the following example; a player knows that she is not hitting the ball well. She is confused about the cause because sometimes she feels that she is swinging too fast, other times it seems that she is taking the club too far inside. She is not sure what is going on but she is sure that it is a mechanical problem. In fact, the mechanical difficulties are the result of the problem, not the *cause*. If a player is not hitting the ball well or having a difficult time staying with a preshot routine, suspect tension as the culprit.

Most often tension starts in the mind. Problems with work, running late to a tee time, and a list of things to do are all common culprits. Unless you are keenly aware you may not know that you are tense, that is, you may not know until it is manifested in your arms, shoulders, and most obviously, your grip pressure.

Recently I completed a study with colleagues in Canada in which we looked at the effects of tension on putting. We increased or decreased tension in moderately skilled putters and looked at how this affected the number of putts made. We also examined the level of brain activity and eye movements during the high and low tension situations. In nearly all cases, we found a strong relationship between tension and putts made. The more tension the fewer putts. This is not too surprising, but we also found out that eye movement and brain waves were also related to tension. The more brain activity the more eye movement, and the more eye movement the fewer putts made. But the story doesn't end there. Through a preshot routine we were able to decrease tension, eye movement, brain activity, and increase putts made.

Many times I have watched a player seem to have a good physical preshot routine, but when I watch more carefully I realized that his eyes were darting around when they should have been focused on the ball. Preshot routines, if done correctly, are very important. One of the reasons for this is that they allow the player to maintain attention without creating tension.

> ### Strength in Limitations
> The human brain can only process one item of information at an instant. This may seem like a limitation of the system but it is in fact great news. If you are paying attention to the right thing, it keeps you from paying attention to the wrong thing. In golf, paying attention to the ball keeps you from paying attention to your thoughts of doom and despair. One trick I have used with my players is to have them read the name of the ball as they are addressing it and as they swing. If they are engaged in reading they cannot be engaged in swing thoughts that get in the way of the swing.

Preshot Routines: *Attention* without *Tension*

If you ever want to check your attention and tension on the course take note of your dwell time. Dwell time is the time that your club dwells (or stays) in address before you actually take the club back. You can have dwell time with any club, including your putter. I am sure you have seen it before; a player stands over the ball during address and seems to freeze like a statue. It seems an eternity passes before they actually take the club back. I have seen it happen so bad that I wanted to touch the person to get them out of it. Every time I see this, it reminds me of the Tin Man in the Wizard of Oz. If you remember the story, at some point the Tin Man freezes because his joints aren't oiled.

I worked with a player once who had a bad case of the Tin Man syndrome. If he did not follow his preshot routine, he would freeze over the ball. He would remain perfectly still for up to seven seconds (I timed him). This was no high handicapper; he was a PGA professional. It wasn't his normal dwell time but something was going on to create it. Just in case you don't think that seven seconds is a long time, try this experiment next time you are at the driving range with a friend. Explain to your friend what you are doing. When you address the ball, the friend will count to himself 1-Mississippi, 2-Mississippi, 3-Mississippi and so on up to 7-Mississippi. When he reaches 7-Mississippi he will say 'go' and you take the club back. If you are like most people, 7-Mississippi will seem like a very long time.

Now an interesting thing happens when you have an excessive dwell time. Even though you are not moving, your internal clock is still going. It is like your internal clock says, "OK, we have 8 seconds to hit the ball." That's 8 seconds from the time to address until you strike the ball. (This time is much shorter for putts.) If you spend seven seconds in dwell time, you only have one second to hit the ball. To do this you must swing very quickly, which in turn creates a whole host of mechanical problems. This is one of the reasons Ben Hogan and others have stated the importance of a waggle. The waggle gives you time to get comfortable over the ball without being frozen. When you are dwelling over the ball in a frozen position one part of you is keeping the club from moving while your internal clock is telling you that you should take the club back. This conflict creates tension and as I have said before, tension is a killer to a good swing.

In the case of the Tin Man, he had drastic differences in results depending on how well he stuck to his preshot routine. On the first day of the tournament he did not stick to it well. After each round I have my players grade themselves on how well they stuck to the routine. On the first day, the Tin Man graded himself a 50% and he shot a 73. He worked hard on the range to make the preshot stronger and was very aware of it on the second day. He graded himself at 85% that second day and he shot a 65. Since that day the player formerly known as the Tin Man has graded no less than 75% in any round. The Tin Man is no longer the Tin Man and he is playing very good golf.

The Tin Man was a case of changing something mental (preshot) which affected something physical. Remember, mental changes can happen quickly and dramatically, but what about the player that stuck to his routine and seemed to be in the game mentally?

The better the treasure map the easier it is to rediscover where you buried the treasure

Rediscovery is directly related to discovery and refinement. The better job you do in these two areas the easier rediscovery will happen. In this sense, rediscovery is a great example of 'pay now or pay later'. If, during discovery, you have video and/or notes of what you discovered to let you play your best golf, you can simply refer to those notes and get back to where you were. Anyone who has played the game knows that there are little things in the game that can make a big difference. These little things can be mental as well as physical. I remember working with a very accomplished player who was getting terribly frustrated with his game. As we talked he mentioned that he was no longer having fun with the game. I asked what the difference was between now and when he had fun.

"When I was a kid I loved to play golf. It was so much fun. It didn't matter where I was on the course, I was looking forward to the next shot. If my approach shot was 50-feet away from the pin I didn't care. I got excited about making a 50-foot putt. My focus was on hitting great shots from anywhere on the course. But it is not that way anymore."

"What is your focus now?" I asked

"Now I seem to always think of where I don't want to hit the ball. I feel restricted in my mindset. I feel like I am avoiding things instead of going for targets."

"How has it served you to avoid things rather than go for targets?" I know this might sound like an odd question but the players and I talk a lot about limiting beliefs and empowering beliefs. Limiting beliefs are those that stand in your way, like the belief that you must avoid trouble. Empowering beliefs are those that empower you to aggressively go for your goals. The difference between limiting and empowering beliefs is like the difference between trying not to lose and trying to win. The difference is huge.

The difference between limiting and empowering beliefs is like the difference between trying not to lose and trying to win. It's huge.

We continued the conversation for a couple of holes. At the end he had made the decision to commit to his empowering beliefs. From then on his game improved leaps and bounds and tournament records fell time after time. By focusing on what he did not want to do, he was getting in his way. By focusing on where he wanted to hit the ball he let his abilities take over.

> "Whether you think you can or you think you can't, you're right."
> *Henry Ford*

Like I said, sometimes rediscovery is not physical, it is mental. When my friend was playing well as a junior golfer, he could have written down his mental state and then he could have referred to that when the game started to go south. But most of us, let alone a junior golfer, do not take the time to document the things we do well. Write it down and you will save yourself a lot of time and frustration in the future.

Although the rediscovery process happened quickly for my friend, it does not always happen this way. Typically, when we rediscover something we must work on it to make it our dominant habit. To do this you can use the techniques discussed in the refinement section. The better you are at refinement the better able you will be in translating rediscovery into your habit.

IT'S NOT JUST PHYSICAL

As we talked about, discovery, rediscovery, and refinement are not only about practicing physical skills; they are also about practicing mental skills. I have worked with many people who have told me that they want to get back to the way they used to think about the game when they were kids. What they are actually telling me is that they want to rediscover the fun of the game.

Two of the best putters on the PGA tour are Brad Faxon and Chris Riley. Faxon has said that he putts best when he doesn't worry about it; when he putts just like he did when he was a kid. He has rediscovered the joy of making putts rather than labor over it like a necessary evil.

Anyone who knows Chris Riley knows he is still a kid at heart and he takes that freedom with him when he putts, but it hasn't always been that way.

When Chris was a junior golfer he was an extremely talented ball striker but only a so-so putter. When he got to college at UNLV, his coach, Dwaine Knight, set out to improve Chris' putting. Coach Knight is a master of putting mechanics, but that wasn't what really turned things around for Chris. Every day when Chris was playing golf, Coach Knight would have the same conversation with him.

"What are you, Chris?" Coach Knight would ask.

Early on in his collegiate career Chris would answer, "I'm one under, Coach." or "I'm not playing well, Coach."

"No, Chris," Coach Knight would say. "You're a great putter."

Eventually, Chris caught on.

"What are you, Chris?" Coach would ask.

Reflexively Chris would say, "I am a great putter." And indeed he is.

Even now, as a winner on the PGA tour and former Ryder Cup player, if Coach Knight, or most anyone for that matter, asked Chris what he is, he will tell you he is a great putter.

Coach Knight knew that for Chris to be a great putter he had to change Chris' belief system in addition to his mechanics. During his college years Coach Knight worked on the discovery and refinement of Chris Riley's belief system, and it worked miraculously.

You should never underestimate the power of belief. It can be one of your most powerful weapons. It can also be one of your most dreaded foes. Belief is something we create. We have a choice in the matter. Unfortunately, more often than not we teach ourselves to believe that we are less capable than we are. Most times we do this without even knowing it. How many times have you hit a bad shot and called yourself stupid, or that you suck, or other self-deprecating remarks? Each time you do that you are teaching yourself negativity. How many times have you hit a good shot and called yourself a great golfer or rewarded yourself for the shot? When you do that you are teaching yourself positivity. It may sound funny to you at first to say such things and "I am a great golfer" or "that was such a great shot", but if you are honest with yourself and truly committed, you will soon become the great golfer you have taught yourself you are.

Just like physical skills, you can teach yourself good mental skills. Many of these skills have already been discussed in the first section. By combining the information from practice with the information from the process you can discover, rediscover, or refine your strong mental skills until they are your strongest weapons.

> ### *Key Points*
>
> ♦ First set your goal of practice as discovery, re-discovery, or refinement and then plan practice based on that goal
>
> ♦ Put aside instant gratification for long term success.
>
> ♦ Show discipline in practice and it will reward you during play
>
> ♦ A good teacher facilitates any goal of practice. A good teacher will also help match your feedback (proprioception) with what is really happening in your swing.

Never underestimate the power of honest belief

Goals become Reality

> "Along with a vision of what he wants, he always has a plan, and he has the patience and understanding and the drive to take all the little steps, says Haney. At the beginning, there are a lot of them and the progress is slow, and everybody is second-guessing him. But eventually there are fewer steps, and things come faster, and then there's a breakthrough like what happened this year. Most people, and a lot of players, don't understand that process. He does."
>
> *- Hank Haney talking about Tiger Woods*
> *(GolfDigest, January 2007, pg 96)*

Now you have all the information you need to work smart and dramatically improve your golf. The only problem is that none of this information will work unless you do. This is where goals come in. Goals, if designed well, give you a road map to your destination and create the momentum to get you there. You may have been over goals before, but what follows is not your normal goal-setting session.

A couple of years ago, Andre Agassi hosted a handful of golfers at one of his restaurants in Las Vegas. We ate and talked for nearly three hours. It was quite extraordinary. I have always viewed Andre as a great tennis player and a great competitor in general, but I never knew him enough to realize his outstanding thoughtfulness and candor. All topics were open for discussion (except his current wife). One of the topics broached that night was goals, or more appropriately, goal-setting.

Goals, of course, are nothing new, at least not to highly successful performers. In fact, it has been estimated that of the top 5% of performers in most all areas of sport and business, nearly all use goals. *"Use"* is the operant word because just having goals is not good enough. The old saying is that goals don't work unless you do. I have studied goals and goal-setting for quite some time, but Andre put a new twist on it for me when he said, *"You may have goals, but remember, life happens between the goals."*

The way I interpreted this was to say, don't sit on your laurels. Don't think just having goals is good enough. Get out there and live your life to make the goals become realities. Look, the truth is that it is not terribly rare for people to have goals. I am sure hundreds of thousands of people have the best of intentions when they write their goals each New Year's day, but intentions alone don't get the job done. Of those people who take the time to write their goals, few take the time to use the goals to guide what they do, and only the highest level performers commit to their goals to guide their day-to-day decisions.

One of the reasons that goals are so important is that they go hand-in-hand with the process of success. This process is part of how you live your life and what you do on a day-to-day basis. The process is part of how you make decisions and respond to the outcomes those decisions create.

I remember one summer when I was young, my father decided we would drive from our home in Dallas to upstate New York. "It will be fun," he kept telling us. So in the Texas heat wave known as July, my seven brothers and sisters and I walked to the van with an attitude and pace that resembled the Baton Death March. The enthusiasm with which we started to sing *99 Bottles of Beer on the Wall* didn't even create enough momentum to take us out of the city. We had a goal that first day to make it to Sequoia National Park in Kansas. This is where the story got a little weird for me.

I won't go into detail about this stop or any other along the two-week ordeal. However, it is worth mentioning that upon arriving in Sequoia, I quickly found out that ticks find very remote areas of the body to dig in. My mother felt that the best remedy for ridding one of a tick was to burn it off. Upon inspection of the tick and where it had buried itself, my mother casually took the cigarette from between her lips and burnt the tick off me. It was not the painless experience she had promised. To this day, I have an issue with cigarettes.

Anyway, back to the story. Each day of the trip, we had a goal of where we wanted to be by the end of the day. Each day between morning and night, life happened. The tick incident is only one of many examples emblazoned into my memory of how life goes on between daily goals. The point is that goals are the destinations we are tying to achieve, but along the way, the process guides our actions.

Goals present the destination, the process presents the means

It would be tough for me or anyone else to sell commitment to the process if the goals are not your own. You have to create your own leverage, your own reason for wanting to achieve your goals. One way to do this is to ask yourself a few simple questions. Take a moment here and, rather than reading the questions, pull out a piece of paper and write down the answers to the following questions. Do it on the back on this book if that's more convenient – just do it. Being physically engaged in the process is a key factor in your level of commitment.

- ♦ What would it feel like if you didn't achieve your goals?
- ♦ How would it affect your life?
- ♦ How will it feel when you do achieve your goals?
- ♦ Will it empower you to achieve more?

The answers to these questions will start changing words into feelings. Feelings are much more likely than words to create momentum. Think of situations in the past where you have decided to act. That decision wasn't brought about by words, it was brought about by feelings. I say this as a person not known to show great emotion. I do know that words can easily go in one ear and out the other, but when you have a feeling about what you want, it seems to hit home much more soundly. Keep this in mind for the rest of the goal chapter.

If you commit to a goal and carry it through, goals can create a great deal of momentum for success in all areas of your life. This isn't just me telling you this. Research on goal-setting has made a strong case that goal-setting consistently facilitates performance. In other words, you can't reach your goals if you don't set them. This is one reason why all the best performers set goals. Think about it this way: If you don't know where you're going, it's pretty difficult to get there.

The Basics of Setting Goals

How you set goals is a critical factor in the likelihood that you will achieve them. Believe me, I have seen many people set goals and rarely have I seen someone do a good job with it. The reason for this is that setting goals correctly requires knowledge of goal-setting fundamentals. To not have the fundamentals would be like asking someone to solve an algebra equation when they don't understand multiplication. Most people don't think of it this way because they believe it is just a matter of writing down what they want to achieve. This is in large part why people often don't achieve what they write down.

Fortunately, once you understand the basic formula for goal-setting, the process is straightforward. Science tells us that when you set goals, it is very important for your goals to be stated in terms of specific, measurable behaviors. Goals such as "I want to do my best" and "I want to do get better" are not very effective because these goals are difficult to measure. Goals such as "I will improve my bench press by 20% by working out three times a week" or "My average putts per round will decrease by practicing an extra 20 minutes a day on putting" are much more effective because they are specific and can be measured.

Research has also shown a direct relationship between goal difficulty and the resulting performance. This means that if a goal is too easy or too difficult, it doesn't help. This is similar to the Challenge Point concept talked about several chapters ago. If a goal is too easy, performance tends not to improve because there was really no challenge for you in the first place. For example, setting a goal of no rounds over 90 is not very motivating for a 2-handicapper. On the other hand, if the goal is extremely difficult or unrealistic, it may lead to frustration and failure. Setting a goal of no rounds over 65 may not be realistic regardless of your ability.

Again, an inappropriate goal will lead to lack of improvement and sometimes the frustration can cause you to go backwards. So choose your goals carefully. Once again, the concept of appropriate challenge (i.e. Challenge Point) comes into play. Appropriately difficult goals are the key to success. If they are too difficult or too easy they will do you little good. Set aggressive yet attainable goals and your performance will rise to a higher level, and then you can set even higher goals.

Be patient but tenacious when it comes to your goals

In no way am I suggesting you sell yourself short. Don't underestimate your ability. Just be realistic, and being realistic is based on your belief. If you truly believe you can decrease your scoring average by two strokes, so be it. But if you only hope you can decrease your scoring average by two strokes, rethink your goals or rethink your limiting beliefs. Set goals that you believe in. They are your goals, so it doesn't matter what others believe, but it does matters what you believe.

A requirement of goal-setting is that you are very honest with yourself when setting goals. One way to do this is once you have written your goals, look at yourself in the mirror and state the goals out loud. You will know in a hurry how you feel about them. If you can't look at yourself in the eye, you know one of two things is happening. (1) Your goal is too easy or too difficult and you know it. (2) Your self beliefs are limiting you and you need to rethink why you let them get in the way of your success.

GOALS 101

The rest of the chapter is divided into two sections. First, you are going to get the full version of goals – how to set them, what types of goals to set, how to carry them out, etc. Second, you will get the short version – a couple of paragraphs that make it all pretty simple. Read the full version to get the big picture, and then read the simple version to see how to make goal-setting your habit.

Short-term and long-term goals

When you set goals keep in mind both *short-term* and *long-term* goals. The short-term goals allow you to see immediate improvements in performance, which in turn keeps you motivated for the long-term goal. It is much easier to stay motivated for a two-week plan than a two-year plan.

One way to think about your goals is to visualize them as a staircase. Your long-term goal is the top of the staircase. Each step along the staircase is a short-term goal. When you complete a short-term goal, you move up one step on the staircase.

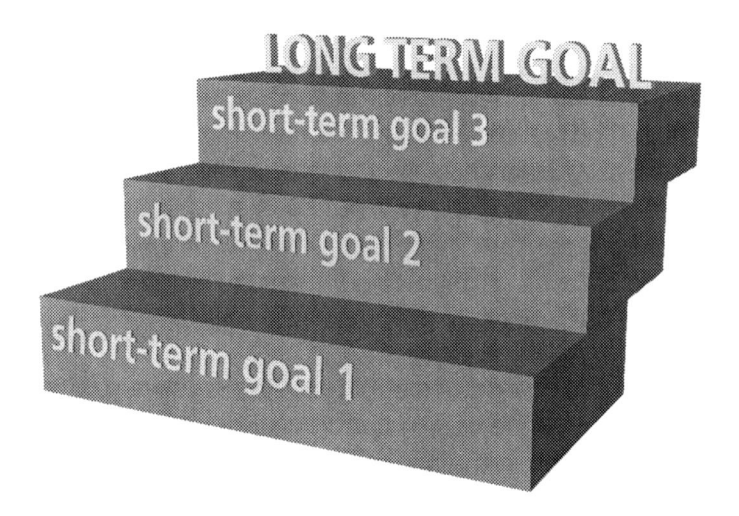

I was first introduced to the idea of a staircase for short-term goals by my son, Max, when he was about seven months old. Max had recently started crawling and one day I watched him crawl to the staircase in our house. For some reason this intrigued me a great deal. Perhaps it was the way he looked at the first step. At the time, the step was slightly lower than his head. On his hands and knees and with very little movement, he stared at it intently. As most adults do, I imagined the conversation he must be having with himself at the time. I pretended it was similar to the conversation Columbus had when he started to sail across the ocean. "I wonder what is on the other side?" In Max's world, he was charting new territory. He had never tried the stairs before.

For the next 2-3 minutes Max worked to climb that first step. He tried a variety of techniques including leg first, head slide on the carpet, and finally, the nearly always successful lunge. He stopped for a moment, and then the next step was assaulted by this great explorer. As I watched him, I noticed that nearly all of his attention was given to the step he was trying to reach, and only occasionally would he look to the top of the staircase. This is the essence of goal setting. Focus on the short-term goals while keeping in mind the prize at the end.

Focus on the short term goals while keeping in mind the prize at the end

Process Goals vs. Result Goals

Within short- and long-term goals, there are process goals and results. (In the literature on goal-setting, these are called *performance* goals and *outcome* goals, respectively.) Differentiating between these types of goals is particularly important in golf. Process goals are things like, "I will focus on each shot." They address aspects of the process rather than focusing on the results. Result goals are things like, "I will win the tournament," and they are focused on the result or outcome of performance.

Process goals are about the present because they direct your attention to what you are doing now. They supply you with the steps that need to be completed to achieve the outcome you choose. Process goals include committing to each shot and staying with your pre-shot routine.

Result goals are about the future. "I will win the tournament" doesn't tell you how to do it, only what to do, but result goals are important because they provide the motivation to focus on the process. In this regard, you can think of the process and result goals just like a recipe and a cake. The process is the recipe; it tells you what you need to do and in what order to get the result you would like. In this case, the result is the cake. Just like Max and the stairs, just like short- and long-term goals, process and result goals provide two steps to the equations. They allow you to simultaneously keep your nose to the grindstone and your eye on the prize.

If you want excellence in your life, choose excellence as a goal. Measure it by every decision you make, no matter how small. For example, when your alarm clock goes off in the morning, do you get out of bed or do you hit the snooze button? Sometimes it is a real challenge to make the choice of excellence, but embracing the challenge rather than fighting it will win you the war.

Embrace the challenge and choose excellence

<table>
<tr><td>

HELPFUL HINT:

Remind yourself of your goals on a daily basis. Write down an abbreviated version of your goals, reminders of them, and read them every day. It will help keep you on track.

</td><td>

Key Points

♦ Set realistic but challenging goals

♦ Set short-term and long-term goals

♦ Be patient but relentless when it comes to your goals

♦ Set process goals more than outcome goals

♦ Remind yourself of your goals and success

</td></tr>
</table>

A FEW EXTRA TRICKS OF THE TRADE

SET LIFESTYLE GOALS

To achieve excellence, you must surround yourself with excellence. Make lifestyle choices a key component of your goals. Goals such as "I will surround myself with people of excellence" are lifestyle goals. It means that the people with whom you choose to associate are people you hold in high esteem. This is important because like attracts like. Play with good golfers and you get better. Play with bad golfers and you don't. One of my favorite stories about this is that of the big dog and the little dog. A friend told me the story a while back, and I think it really hits home.

BIG DOG, LITTLE DOG

An old man was sitting on his porch with head in hand. Clearly he was distressed as his grandson approached.

"Grampa, what's wrong?" the boy queried.

"I keep watching the fight between the big dog and the little dog. I have watched it all my life and it wears on me," the old man replied.

"Grampa, I didn't know you had dogs. I've never seen them," the boy remarked.

"That is because they are in my head. One dog represents everything I am ashamed of. All the decisions I have made out of insecurity, jealousy, and fear. The other dog represents everything I am proud of. All the good decisions I have made out of courage and honor. The two dogs fight and fight and they have been doing it for years. The biggest dog always wins."

"Which one is the big dog, good or bad?" the boy asks.

The old man replied, "Which ever one I feed."

Everybody feeds a dog. Which one they feed tells a lot about them. It is important to know that when a person is feeding their dog they are also whetting the appetite of yours. There are only two choices. The people with whom you associate either help you toward your goals or hurt you. There is no neutral. If you are feeding a dog, it is either good or bad. There is no neutral dog. The same goes for the people around you, so choose your role models carefully.

A *Role Model* is a person who serves as your counsel, either literally or figuratively, and they serve two purposes. First, they can provide advice or guidance. Second, they can compress time.

Role models serve two purposes: they can provide advice or guidance, and they can compress time

The literal role model is a person you go to with questions of "What would you do?" This type of role model is obviously someone you know. For example, I have a friend who bought a business in the late 1990's when he was 27. He bought the business for a little less than $400,000. He worked hard to build the business and approximately eight years later he sold it for $22 million. He bought another business, built it, sold it, and so on. His most recent project is a series of high rises in Las Vegas.

At the point I am writing this, he has sold more than $44 million worth of his properties. My friend will turn 40 in two years. When I have a question about risk taking, he is the one I talk to. He is my literal entrepreneur role model and as such, he provides guidance and advice. In addition to answering questions about specific projects or investments, my friend also has the ability to compress time, at least for me. When I talk to him, I am the fortunate recipient of years of his knowledge. In a two-hour lunch meeting he can teach me many of the things it took him 15 years to learn. He is the equivalent of Cliff Notes for *Moby Dick*.

Not all role models have to be a person you know, and hence the figurative role model. This is a person that you would think, "What would they do?" For example, Herm Edwards is the head coach of the Kansas City Chiefs. I've never met him, but I have seen him many times on television interviews. One of the things that has always struck me about Coach Edwards is that he takes responsibility for his actions and he never allows excuses.

On occasion, I have used Coach Edwards as my discipline role model. For example, one day I was feeling a bit lazy and was going to skip my workout, but there, in my mind's eye, Coach Edwards was riding on my shoulder like the good angel of the good/bad angel team. Coach Edwards didn't say a word but just shook his head with a disgusted look on his face. This virtual Coach Edwards knows one of my goals is to be in good shape and he wasn't going to let me make an excuse to get in the way of my goal.

Choose someone you respect to be your role model and it will clarify which decision is the right decision. As I stood at the crossroads between having a beer and going on a run, all I needed to do was see Coach Edwards and knew the decision I should make. This same philosophy works for most any goal you have. If you would like, choose different role models for different goals. You may have one for your fitness goals, one for your financial goals, and one for your golf goals. Likewise, if you want to be a great putter, find a great putter and ask him to share his secrets. Golf is one of the few games where competitors will help each other.

In 2006 I was at the FBR Phoenix Open with one of my players. It was the day before the first tournament round. Between the practice green, chipping area, and driving range nearly every pro was practicing. Between the 80 or so players and hundreds of spectators, there was quite a bit of commotion for a practice day. All of a sudden, a great deal of attention was focused at one of the practice bunkers. Jeff Sluman was giving five or six players a lesson in bunker play. That's right; the day before he was to compete against these guys, he was helping them get better. Sluman was being a role model for bunker play and he was being a role model for sportsmanship.

Who are your role models?

Who will help you feed the good dog?

SHORT AND SIMPLE SUGGESTIONS

SET PRACTICE GOALS AS WELL AS TOURNAMENT GOALS

Take a few minutes before each practice to set goals. Many of my players use a rating system to assess their putting. For example, if they are working on staying in a putt (keeping their head down) they may rate how well they did on a 1-10 scale (with 10 being perfect). So, a practice session goal may be, "I will have an 8 or better rating on each putt." If you don't use such a system, you may set other goals. For example, if you are working on chipping and you have three or four spots picked out around the green from which you are chipping, you may have a goal of making three chip-ins from each spot around the green. Go into each practice session with a purpose.

Go into each practice session with a purpose

STATE GOALS IN A POSITIVE FASHION

State the goals in the positive. For example, "I will make 3-foot putts" is better than "I won't miss any 3-foot putts." By stating goals in a positive fashion, you teach yourself a different method of thinking. You are trying to make a putt rather than protecting against missing a putt. Additionally, this phrasing enhances the attitude of belief. "I will make 3-foot putts" helps create your belief in your ability.

IDENTIFY TARGET DATES FOR ATTAINING GOALS

When you set a goal, be sure to set a date by which the goal will be achieved. This will make it real and there becomes a measurable objective. If you meet your goal on or before the target date, reward yourself by setting another goal and the next target date. Goals are dynamic in that they change as you do. If you have not yet met your goals, figure out why and remedy it by your next deadline.

WRITE DOWN YOUR GOALS AND SET UP A SCORING SYSTEM

Set up a scoring system for each goal. A 1-10 rating usually works for this. Rate yourself each time and chart your progress. Post the goals achieved on your refrigerator or bulletin board. Take pride in what you have accomplished. That pride will help you develop momentum and will help you accomplish even more.

GET FEEDBACK ABOUT YOUR GOALS

Go over your goals with someone you trust and ask them to give you feedback about how you are doing. I like to call this person a *Goal Keeper*. A Goal Keeper is someone who will hold up the mirror for you and holds you accountable for your actions. They help keep you on track and encourage you. You know where you want to be, your Goal Keeper shows you whether or not you are making the right decisions to get there. Get the right people on your team and get the wrong people off. You choose who you deal with. "I will surround myself with people who will feed the good dog" is a good goal statement for this. Look around and see if the key people in your life are helping or hurting. Think of it as if all the key people in your life are paddling a boat. If everyone is paddling the same way, the boat moves well. If one person is paddling against the others, the boat is not moving smoothly. Find out if anyone is paddling against the rest. If they are, give them the option of turning around or stepping off.

GOLDILOCKS AND GOALS

Time and time again we have talked about the optimal challenge and Goldilocks. Goals fit into this as well. You want just the right number of goals – not too many or too few. This can be accomplished by choosing 2-3 main goals, and the rest will come along for the ride. For example, if one of your goals is to work out four times a week, you don't have to have additional goals of losing weight, eating better, and running 10 miles a week. These things will happen if you stick to your major goal. Additionally, these secondary goals may be part of what is called the GPA, as discussed at the end of this chapter.

Choose 2-3 main goals. The rest will come along for the ride

CREATE LEVERAGE

This is not my suggestion. I heard it from Tony Robbins of the Robbins Research Institute. Tony is one of the best motivational speakers I have ever had the privilege of hearing. One of the many areas of strength he possesses is goal-setting and fulfillment. I think that one of the things that sets him apart from others who espouse a goal-setting philosophy is that he understands the power of leverage.

In this case, leverage is the means to create urgency and motivation. Think about it this way: It is difficult to move a large rock by just trying to lift it or push it with your bare hands. However, if you use a pole wedged underneath the rock as leverage, the rock will move quite easily. Goals work the same way. Find the leverage, and you will move anything standing between you and your goal.

> ### Key Points
>
> ♦ Choose a Goal Keeper as part of your support environment
> ♦ Make lifestyle goals so good choices become your habit
> ♦ Phrase goals positively for practice and play
> ♦ Keep track of your achievement

You have now completed Goal Setting 101. The next short section is the crib notes. The take-home message can be largely captured in three letters: GPA. The principles of Goal Setting 101 are still in place, but the method can be streamlined through the simple formula presented below.

Goal, Plan, Action (GPA)

The process of setting a goal, plan, and action is one of the simplest but most powerful habits you can have. If you follow a few simple rules you will be able to make anything you do much more efficient and much more likely to succeed. Goal, plan, and action, abbreviated GPA, is just like it sounds.

First you need to set a goal, then develop a plan to accomplish the goal, and finally action is required. Although there are volumes written about how to set goals (including in this book), the process is really pretty simple if you start at the end. Picture what you want to be or what you want to happen. Have a very clear vision of the outcome you want. See every detail, including what you look like and feel like when you have accomplished your goal. Spending just 30-60 seconds with this process will create a great deal of leverage. Understand where you are going and you will be much more likely to get there. Most people skip this step. They think of the words of what they want to achieve but they never see it, they never feel it.

See it and you are on your way. Feel it and it will be yours.

After you have a very clear picture of your goal, create the plan to get there. If you want to be a great putter, think of the actions you will need to create what you want. It may mean seeing a putting coach, or practicing for 30 minutes a day on specific drills, or having a different mindset about putting in general. Be very specific here. "I will practice extra" doesn't get it. "Each day I will practice speed drills for 30 minutes" is much better. Just like the goal, take 30 seconds and see what you will be doing.

The final step in this part of the equation is the action. Carry out the plan you have developed. Evaluate how well you did using a "good, better, how" method. This method was actually created by The First Tee as part of their teaching method. Using the method, the person being evaluated states what was good about the experience, what could be better, and how to make it better. This same method can be used in any assessment technique to create a constructive evaluation and future plan. For example, if the plan is, "Each day I will practice speed drills for 30 minutes," the good, better, how might be as follows:

GOOD: "It was good to spend that time practicing, and I can tell it is helping my speed."

BETTER: I can be more efficient and learn faster. I can be more focused.

HOW: I will have a plan before I get to the putting green. I will have a clear vision of what I want to be like as a putter before I step in the green.

When you exercise the GPA on a regular basis, it becomes your habit and because it is your habit, it happens with very little effort. The more practiced you are at developing GPAs, the better your GPA will be and the better the outcome will be.

The GPA can serve for short-term and long-term goals. In fact, many good golfers use short-term GPAs without even knowing about it. For example, each time they hit a chip shot they have a GPA. Perhaps the goal is to leave the ball just below the hole. The plan involves club selection, ball flight (bump and run or lofted shot), and where the ball will land. Like with other goals, seeing it increases the chances of being it. They picture the shot and rehearse it until it's right. The action is performing the shot.

With this in mind, how often do you have a GPA? My guess is that the more often you do, the more often you are successful, and when you don't have a plan for what you want, you don't often get the result you would like. Like I said, the better the GPA, the more likely you will have a good result. It has been my experience that when people hit a bad chip or shot, there are some common reasons. Ask them what they were thinking and you will hear things like: I didn't want to hit it too hard, I didn't want to leave it short, I guess I wanted it to go in, what do you mean? I don't know what I was thinking.

Rarely will you hear of a GPA gone bad. Instead, these answers seem to have two things in common. First, they are phrased in the negative with words like "didn't." They talk about what they didn't want to do rather than what they did want to do. Second, their target, or focus, was pretty general. That is, they were not very specific about what they wanted to do. If you are 15 feet from the pin and you don't want to hit it too hard, that leaves over 14 feet of acceptable error. In my mind, that is far too much acceptable error.

Now, if you counter what high handicappers say versus low handicappers, you will notice a few important differences. The low handicapper will replace the don'ts with dos. I wanted to leave it below the hole, I wanted it to trickle off the slope to the hole, I wanted to bump a wedge into the hill and let it die. But when they fail, they will generally tell you that they weren't committed to the shot. In other words, they did not have a good GPA.

One of the differences between good golfers and the best golfers is that the best can be very creative with their GPA and they have complete belief that their goals will become reality. For most any player, the more committed they are to their GPA, the more likely it will work. This is true for a chip shot or a 5-year plan. Commitment to the GPA is a major component in the process. Leverage, vision, and a great GPA will go a long way to helping you achieve anything you desire.

> ### *Key Points*
>
> ◆ The better your GPA, the more likely you will have a good result
>
> ◆ Commitment to the GPA is a major component in the process
>
> ◆ Your GPA is an ongoing process. Finish one, revise and go again. Keep recycling the GPA until you achieve the long-term goal you were looking for.

Supercharged Learning

> If club manufacturers can use rocket science to build a better golf club why can't we use brain science to build a better golfer?

Sometimes revelations come to us in a roundabout way, and it's not uncommon for it to take time for these revelations to unveil themselves. When I was a graduate student I remember a conversation with one of my professors about the research project we were working on. The project was designed to understand how humans process information. That is, how we take in information, decide what to do with it, and finally execute a response. The topic, know as stimulus-response compatibility, was quite hot at the time, at least among Cognitive Psychologists. The problem was that I didn't have a clear picture of how our research could be applied to help people. Much to my surprise my professor was quite irritated that I thought that any research we did should have a practical application. The conversation was finished when he informed me that "We do research because there are theoretical questions to answer. We do not do research so that people can use it." At this point a seed was planted that festered for a few years before it took root. It never sat well with me that the answers we get from research could, and generally do, stay in the ivory towers of the university. In fact, this seed turned into revelation, shaped my research for the next twenty years and continues to do so.

From that day on I paid attention to how long it took research findings to work their way to the general public. I was amazed and disappointed that in many cases it took years, and unfortunately, some pretty interesting findings never got to see the light of day. By the time a discovery was made the scientist was on to the next question and unless you were in the habit of reading scientific journals, you probably would never hear about it. The good news is that some of this has changed in recent years. Just to put this in perspective, when I had that original conversation with my professor we were still a few years away from the source of rapid fire information overload known as the Internet.

> ### The Google Generation
> Not long ago my six-year-old son Max and five-year-old daughter Ali were having a conversation. Truth be told, they were having an argument that had advanced enough to be at the "did not-did too" stage. I intervened by telling them that they would settle nothing by "did not-did too" and they either needed to get more information or stop arguing. Max said to Ali, "OK then, let's Google it." And off they went.

Prior to the Google generation, information from science was very slow in coming. Even so, typing in phrases like "Neuroscience and Golf" to any search engine, including Google, still gives you little usable information. The reason for this is that to use information someone still needs to translate from science to application. Just having information is not enough. It has to be usable, and this is where the very good news of modern science comes in. There is quite a bit of information in the cognitive neuroscience field that can be applied to golf. Although this information was not designed to understand golf, it does provide us with tremendous insights into how learning takes place, and this information can be translated in to learning golf. The application of neuroscience to golf is where we are going with this supercharged learning chapter.

Now that you have read most of this book you know that there are two basic ways to practice. One is set up for elaboration, or deep learning, and the other is set up for forgetting (rote repetition), and each has its place in the grand scheme of how to practice golf. Pure repetition is used for *discovery* and little for *re-discovery*, but beyond that you will be wasting your time if all you do is mindlessly hit balls. On the other hand, if you actually want to create efficient learning you can use elaboration. In fact, at this time you might guess that elaboration is the real key to the learning equation, and your guess would be partially correct. Elaboration works well for refinement and it helps with the rediscovery process as shown in the summary table below.

Summary Of The Types Of Practice And Types Of Memory

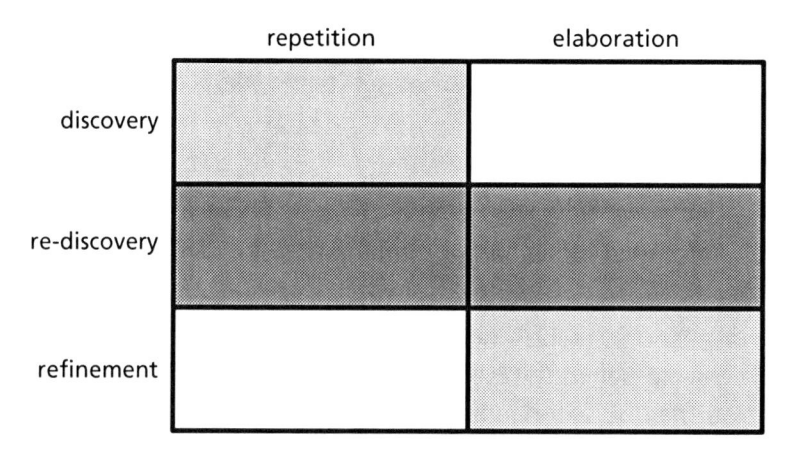

Table 1. A list of the practice goals (discovery, re-discovery, and refinement) paired with the types of practice to facilitate the goal. For example, for discovery repetition is useful whereas repetition alone is not useful for elaboration.

Setting practice goals and using the methods that facilitate those goals is a great way to increase what you get out of each practice session. The idea is that to get you where you want to go you need two things: (1) You need to know where you want to go and (2) you need to choose the proper vehicle to get you there. If you don't have both you will not be efficient. Obviously choosing a boat to get from Las Vegas to Los Angeles is not a good idea. This same idea holds true in the final chapter on learning. Keep in mind all that you have learned so far and the rest of this chapter will be the keystone to your best golf.

RELEVANCE

Recent findings in neuroscience have taught us that there is yet another level that can create supercharged learning. I call this level *relevance*, and this is simplest and most fun level of all. The table below shows how relevance fits into the general equation.

Summary Of The Types Of Practice And Types Of Memory

	repetition	elaboration	relevance
discovery			
re-discovery			
refinement			

Table 2. Relevance supercharges refinement but it can also trigger re-discovery.

So you have read this whole book and now we get to supercharged learning. Now we get to the 'simplest and most fun level of all.' At this point you may be wondering why I didn't give you the best way to learn first and skip all the rest of what we have talked about. There is a simple reason for this and it is a theme used many times through the book. You should be challenged at the appropriate level and this includes the time and place to get information. The types of practice we have discussed thus far are important and they are fundamental in developing a strong mental and physical base for your golf. You must understand the basics of efficient and inefficient learning as part of your foundation and these methods will continue to be used. Master the foundation and the rest of the structure will withstand any blow. Have a shaky foundation and it will crumble with the slightest sign of strain.

In addition to what you have already learned, *relevance*, the last aspect of learning, is the Lamborghini of learning. It is not something to be taken lightly. You need to earn your way to it. Think of it this way, before you go out and buy a Lamborghini it would probably be a good idea to learn to drive. Everything in the book so far was getting you ready for your new Lamborghini.

As you know from earlier chapters on elaboration, meaning creates memories. Relevance is a supercharged way to attach meaning to what you are trying to learn. To understand how it works let's take a very quick visit into the brain, and specifically into an area that ties emotion to memory.

A SHORT TOUR OF THE BRAIN

Emotion and memory go hand in hand when it comes to learning. When I first hear this I thought it meant that if you were not an emotional person you would have trouble learning. This didn't sit well with me, partly because I'm not much on emotion in general. I'm a guy after all and I am in control of my emotions. However, as I studied more I came to understand that 'emotion' is not so much about crying or not at a movie like *Brian's Song*, it is actually more about the juice that we get from situations and the relevance our brain places on certain occurrences. Without even knowing this you have probably already realized it.

Let's say you go to a party and over the course of the evening you meet 10 people. Obviously you won't remember all 10 the next day, and depending on the nature of the party you may have trouble remembering any of them. But let's say you do remember one or two. Which ones do you remember? Is there a pattern to the ones you remember or is it just random luck?

If you are like most people you will remember the person (or people) you find attractive or unique. You will remember the smoking hot flight attendant who flirted with you, or the man who had a mole on his forehead that looked like a third eye. In other words, you will remember those people who stirred emotions in you but you won't remember the ones who had no relevance. The people you remember and the reasons you remember them are no accidents. The brain is specifically set up to remember certain things and forget others, and it's all based on emotional juice.

The "limbic system," which is right in the center of your brain, is in charge of transferring information into memory. This system uses emotion to tune memories. For example, you make a four foot putt. Do you remember it? If it has emotion tied to it chances are you will remember it. If the putt was to win the U.S. Open it has a lot of emotion tied to it. This emotion turns the volume up on the memory and you won't forget it in a million years. However, if the putt was during practice and it was no big deal one way or the other emotion turns the volume down and the putt is likely to be forgotten. This basic understanding is a very powerful ally in remembering, or forgetting, shots on the course.

> ### HOW DO WE KNOW WHAT WE KNOW?
> From years of experiments and the occasional botched brain surgery, we now know that the main structure in charge of transferring information is a portion of the temporal lobe called the hippocampus, but the hippocampus does not do the job by itself. Memories are weighted by emotions (through the interplay between the hippocampus and amygdala). In other words, if something causes our emotions to kick in, the brain basically says "Oh, this must be important." and the memory is saved with more weight or permanence. The more emotion is involved (to a point) the more relevant the information will seem. Relevance and emotion increase memory, and there is a very good reason the brain is set up this way.

Relevance causes permanence

THERE'S A REASON WE'RE SET UP THIS WAY

Let me introduce you to a friend, Milfred, or "Mindless Milfred" to his friends. He's not the sharpest tool in the toolbox if you know what I mean. Milfred decided to go on a guided African safari. As you can imagine it was hot in Africa and so the safari group decided to take a break under a baobab tree. Since Milfred hadn't seen any animals yet and the heat apparently didn't bother him, he decides to do a little exploring on his own. Off Milfred goes walking through tall grass toward a stand of tress. In the tall grass, he sees something with black and yellow stripes stirring about 10 feet in front of him. His primitive brain takes over. This is the lower brain that evolved a long time ago for protection. Without knowing what it is in the grass Milfred's fight or flight response kicks into action to protect him from possible danger. Milfred feels his heart pounding and he freezes, his eyes focused on the stirring in the grass. For a few seconds he is unable to move. Finally, his higher brain (or in Milfred's case slightly higher brain) kicks in and against most people's better judgment Milfred overrides his primitive brain and decides to see what is in the grass. Fortunately for Milfred there are no tigers in Africa. It turns out that it wasn't a wild animal at all but a supermodel who fell asleep in the grass after a photo shoot. She, like Milfred, was not the sharpest tool in the toolbox if you know what I mean. The rest of the crew was in the stand of trees for shade.

The story doesn't end there. A few days later Milfred is again walking along the tall grass and again sees something moving in the tall grass. Before he has time to think about the supermodel he once again feels his heart pounding and he freezes. Once again his primitive brain has taken over. Why? Because better safe than sorry his primitive brain says. Its job is to protect Milfred. When we are in these situations of possible danger our fear response takes over to protect us, and that fear response is much faster and more powerful than normal conscious thought. That fear response is the same thing that can take over on the golf course as well. In fact, it might be even worse on the golf course.

If the stripes in the grass had been an animal that attacked Milfred his emotional memory would have stored general information that would impact him significantly. Tall grass, stripes, sudden movements would all be triggers to this emotional memory. They don't have to be the same grass or the same stripes. The primitive brain only works in generalities and fuzzy pictures. Anytime any of these stimuli were present Milfred's fear response would kick in. The same thing happens for some golfers who have had bad experiences on the course. A bad experience with water elicits emotional memory. The next time that golfer has a shot over water the primitive brain may kick the fear factor in causing all sorts of problems. Remember, it doesn't have to be the same water. The primitive brain works in abstractions.

I'll grant you that this does not yet sound like good news, but it is. You can use this information to your advantage with just a slight twist. You can use the automatic systems of the brain to help you rather than hurt you.

So you see, the more emotional the event the more likely the brain will store this

> ### Divining Rod
> I had a friend who claimed that even though he was not much of an outdoorsman, he would be the person you would want along if you were stranded in the desert. "Give me golf club and I will find water," he boasted.

information with great strength. Therefore, emotional memories cause supercharged learning.

> ### *FEAR FACTOR AND THE YIPS*
>
> By repeating a negative behavior and engraining it into memory, primitive or not, you are creating a fear factor. A fear factor elicits the fight or flight response including a racing heart beat, increased muscle tone, and increased respiration. Fear factors can occur either in logical or illogical settings. Sometimes the fear factor is a reflexive response. You have experienced this if you have ever seen a small rock bounce off the pavement toward your windshield as you are driving. The natural tendency it to move your head to avoid the rock even though there is little chance it will penetrate the windshield. There is good reason for this. One of our brain's primary jobs is protection, even if it means a few false alarms along the way. The cost of incorrectly assuming the rock will come thought the windshield is much less expensive than not moving and the rock coming through the windshield. Other situations are more deliberate. After watching a scary movie it is common to be frightened of a dark house or things that go bump in the night. The same dark house or random sound causes even greater fear if you or someone you know was recently robbed or attacked. Although less devastating to everyday life, the same notion of fear factor can translate to golf. Specifically, it may translate to the yips.
>
> The yips are generally described as involuntary motions of the hand or wrist that can make putting very difficult. The yips can also affect the full swing although it is less common. It is likely that the yips result from anxiety related brain activity, similar to other examples of fear factor. However, if the behavior is repeated frequently enough it can eventually become a conditioned response. To reverse this effect, very deliberate measures must be taken. Our own research has shown that if you can calm the mind you can calm the yips. We use a 'da-da' technique to calm the mind, which in turn calms the eyes and the hands. If our findings are correct, the cure for the yips is far short of a frontal lobotomy.

How does this knowledge of the primitive brain and neuroscience help you with golf? If you engage the same parts of the brain that engage emotion and memory together in a positive way you will supercharge learning. In this case, you will supercharge how quickly you learn a new technique or a new mindset on the course. What used to take weeks or maybe months can now be done in days.

One of the simple ways to cause emotions is to put a cost/reward on the outcome. From here on this cost/reward will be known as *Relevance*. Imagine placing a 2x6 piece of wood on the ground and then walking from one end to the other. I am sure you will be able to walk along the board quite easily. I am also sure that once you have completed this rather mundane task you will wonder what the point is, and except for the curiosity about why you just walked along a board, the activity is quite forgettable. However, imagine walking across the same piece of wood, but now it is suspended between two rooftops 50 feet in the air. Although it is the same piece of wood it is not the same task. Now there is a consequence to your action and the memory of that event will be quite pronounced. The same thing happens in golf.

Let me ask you, have you ever been by yourself on a practice green and missed a short putt, say 3-feet? I would guess that you think you have missed a three foot putt during practice but you can't remember a specific time, or at the very least it is difficult to remember. Now, shift your thoughts to an actual round of golf, perhaps during a tournament. Can you remember missing a short putt during the round? Did the putt affect the round? In both cases it is just a short putt, but the detail and depth of memory for each is remembered entirely different. In fact, it wouldn't surprise me if you had a difficult time remembering any missed short putt during practice even though you have had many. On the other hand, you can probably remember in excruciating detail the last 3-footer you missed in a tournament. This is because relevance causes permanence.

Knowing this, the important questions are how do you add consequence to your golf practice and when do you do it? Once more we run into a bit of good fortune. It turns out that there are lot of ways to add relevance and many of these I am sure you have already done. For example, most people play golf with a side bet or two on the game. Generally, the bet is of little financial significance but it 'makes the game more interesting.' This adds a little more significance to each shot and provides a greater opportunity for learning. Is this a good thing? Maybe, maybe not. The thing to remember about this is by adding emotion you add relevance and that increases memory strength. That may sound good but what if the memory you have is one that you would rather not have? What if you are playing for money and you top the ball off the first tee? If the emotions are high there is a strong likelihood that you will have a clear memory of this on your next tee shot and the next time you play for money. Obviously you would rather not have a clear memory of that. This is the reason you need to develop a strong foundation of skill and confidence before you use relevance, and hence the reason for all the chapters that proceeded this one. As we have already discussed, in some phases of learning you want success and in others you want challenges. When you supercharge learning you want much more success than failure because you have no choice but to remember.

> **REMINDER: PHASES OF LEARNING**
> 1. Very early in learning create success by creating simple tasks
> 2. Transition into less success and more challenge until there is a strong foundation of skill and confidence
> 3. Supercharge learning with emotion

A little later in this chapter we will talk about how to deliver first aid when you have a bad experience in a supercharged setting, but for now let's concentrate on the good news part of the equation.

> **TWO NOTES**
> **(1)** I am not suggesting that you should always be emotional when you are practicing or playing golf. Pick and choose your battles.
> **(2)** Remember that there are times when you want to remember (Refinement) and times when you do not want remember (Discovery). Use the tool of relevance only when it should be used.

TECHNIQUES FOR SUPERCHARGING

> *There is no doubt that people have a difficult time performing when the pressure is on. They practice with no consequences and play with lots of them. The system isn't set up to perform well under these circumstances.*

Use the techniques in this book to be confident and uncomfortable. That's right, you need to be uncomfortable but you need to do it in a way that you know it is helping you. This lack of comfort is like eating vegetables you don't really like. It may not feel good now but it is good for you. I'll bet that if you knew eating broccoli would cut a few shots off your next round you would eat broccoli. Make yourself uncomfortable during practice because for the most part, the more uncomfortable you are, the more potential you have for learning. I don't say this lightly. It will take quite a bit of fortitude to stay on track when you are not hitting the ball well or when you seem to be missing a lot of putts.

Many of the techniques I discuss in this book have been researched on and off the course. In fact, when I get a new idea I test it in the lab and on myself before I take it to the golfers with whom I work. This is true as well for the idea of consequences, and I found out in a hurry if it worked. I went to the course to work on a swing move I had just started learning the day before. I tested it on the range and had the general idea but needed to refine it. I wasn't sure where the ball was going to go with each swing but I needed to work on technique and trust. The range was Level I consequence but I felt that I needed to move to Level II consequence. I had been researching the topic for a while and decided that taking the swing to the course would supercharge learning. This meant that there was a cost or consequence to a bad shot such as losing a ball, frustration, or a poor score. Just as I was leaving the range one of my clients (a very good player) asked if he could play with me. Even as I accepted the invitation I could feel it move me to Level III consequence. Now my normal on course consequences would be seen by someone else. Granted, I was fairly comfortable with the other person but nobody likes to show their dirty laundry in public. As we made our way to the putting green a second client and his coach approached us. The coach was a senior instructor at the Butch Harmon Academy and a very good golfer. I knew him by reputation and had only met him once. They too asked to join us. This ratcheted up the Level III consequence to a Level IV consequence. I played nine holes with the three of them working on my new move and struggling to maintain focus on the process rather than the outcome. I won't lie, it was tough. I had to constantly remind myself what my goal was and what I was learning. In hindsight I might have over-challenged myself from a technique perspective but I learned a great deal about myself mentally. The next day when I went out to practice, the move was orders of magnitude better than it had been the day before. It was difficult but worth it.

Get uncomfortable when it doesn't really matter and you will be more comfortable when it does

TECHNIQUES FOR THE PRACTICE RANGE

Practice with consequence. As you know when most people practice hitting balls a bad shot has very little consequence. For most people, if they hit a bad shot they just use the hit and rake method for the next one. Using this method there is no real purpose to what they are doing. On the other hand, assigning consequence to each shot, good or bad, will raise the emotional value of each shot. This in turn will raise the relevance and the probability of learning. There are several ways to do this. If you are practicing by yourself you can assign reward and punishment to your practice. Take the following practice scenario as an example:

Practice Scenario I (1 hour on full swing)

9:00-9:10 am - check GAPS, grip, alignment, and posture. Hit 10-12 wedges with tempo in mind. Take your time but pay no attention where the ball is going. Keep your mind and your eyes on the spot underneath the ball (which is the divot after you hit). Say 'da-da' or '1-2' to keep a good tempo.

9:10-9:30 am – play 3 ball 5 ball. Whatever you are practicing that day hit 3 to 5 balls in a row and then step away. By this time you should be pretty good at the drill. Try to hit 3 shots exactly the same and when you do switch clubs and targets. Take your time with each shot. Remember, this is elaboration.

9:30-9:35 am – Write it down. Take 5 minutes and write down what you have learned. If you have time left over get some water and stretch a little. Take a couple of tempo swings just like you are on the first tee.

9:35-9:55 am – Consequence drill. Pick a game based on what you need to work on that day and then pick a consequence that means something to you. If you want to work on your driver, play a game where you imagine a narrow fairway on the driving range. One way to play the game is that each drive you drive the ball in the virtual fairway you receive a credit in the reward column, and each time you miss you are docked a credit. For example, the reward may be to go out to dinner. Each time you hit a drive in your virtual fairway you get a point. One point equals one star in the restaurant of your choice. It you earn four points you get to go to a 4-star restaurant. So if you hit 7 out of 10 drives in the fairway you get a 4-star restaurant (7 credits – 3 debits). Six out of 10 is a 1-star restaurant. If you think you are ready to turn up the heat and make it a bit more uncomfortable, play the game with three in a row. In this version you have to hit three drives in a row into your virtual fairway. If you miss one, you get no points. Now to go to a 4-start restaurant you need to hit 12 out of 12 drives in the fairway. You have to be honest here. If you hit two out of three drives in the fairway you get no points and no restaurant.

When I play these consequence games I like to reward good performance rather than punish for bad performance. It provides a positive spin to practice and this tends to put pressure on while still maintaining the positive mindset as you go. The most important point is to make each shot matter.

9:55-10:00 am –Tempo drills as always. Take a short iron and hit a few shots with ¾ swings. Always remind yourself of a good tempo. It can save you when other things are a bit off.

The same games you play by yourself you can play with a partner, plus, the partner brings in even more options. You can play closest to the pin, longest drive, most accurate drive, best wedge shot, or a host of other games on the driving range or practice green. There is nothing new about playing these types of games during practice but when you add consequence to the game it changes the learning opportunity.

Make practice count by adding consequence.

THE GAME WITHIN A GAME

If you want to work on your game in general pick a game at random. One way to do this is to use a dice game to decide on drills. Before you go to practice make three lists from 1 to 6. The first is a list of games. For example, play a game where the goal is to land the ball on one of the driving range greens (or an area that would be the green). Your list can include practice knock down shots, working the ball from left to right, or anything else you want to refine. Write them down 1 to 6 and roll the dice. What ever number comes up that is the game of the day. The second list has the reward if you are successful. Take yourself to dinner, take yourself to the movies, have a beer. Choose whatever motivates you. Roll the dice and that number is your reward. The third roll is your punishment. Extra time on the treadmill, no beer tonight, 5 minute earlier wake up call for each missed shot.

TECHNIQUES FOR THE COURSE

Let's face it, for most people playing most rounds, there is little consequence to a good or bad score. Everybody would rather play well than badly, but for the most part the worst that happens when you play badly is you sulk for a few hours and have an extra cocktail. Now you can use these inconsequential rounds to your advantage. You can add consequence to the 'practice' rounds so you perform better on the rounds that really matter to you. Listed below are four great ways to add consequence.

Challenge yourself in 'practice'; see the rewards in competition.

PLAY WITH STRANGERS - I know, you have been taught all your life to not play with strangers. The reason is that strangers can be dangerous, and now this is exactly the reason you want to play with strangers. Playing a round of golf with people you don't know can be intimidating. The cost of potential embarrassment can be quite high which in turn can add emotion to your game. If you play and are successful, you supercharge learning in a very positive way.

USE YOUR GOOD BALL ON A WATER HOLE – every once in a while I get to play golf with my brother-in-law. He carries an 18 handicap and when we play there is nothing on the line. We agree to just 'play for fun.' (unbeknownst to my brother-in-law I still set up my own consequence schedule). Every time we come to a hole with water on it he pulls out his "water ball." Now I know that most of you know what a water ball is. It is the ball you don't mind losing when it goes in the water. This is probably a good idea for my brother-in-law but if you want to challenge yourself (and maintain USGA rules) I recommend using a regular ball. In fact, if you have a special ball, play with that.

OUT OF BALLS - One of the games you can play by yourself on the course is to play with a limited number of golf balls. This will definitely add consequence to your round. For example, next time you go to play only carry two golf balls with you. If you lose them both you are done, even if you are only 10 or 11 holes into the round. This way, every shot has a consequence.

3-BALL - I realize that most of the time people don't get a chance to practice on the course where they get to hit two or three shots to a hole. However, if the opportunity every presents itself, 3-ball is a great on course practice technique. It is easiest to do this on a par-3. Each player hits one shot, and then a second and a third, alternating who hits next. Play out each ball and the low cumulative score wins. It is a great way to add consequence to the game and if you have to wait on slow play, a great way to pass the time. (You can do this on the practice range as well by picking a 'closest to' target rather than a hole.) You can also play this game using two out of three shots rather than all three, and for higher handicappers this is a good idea.

HUMILITY – Two of my good friends happen to be golf pros. Their nicknames and I kid you not, are 'Poop' and 'Bone.' I did not give them these names nor will I go into how the names came into being. Regardless, the two are very good friends and good players and have created a game called *Humility*. The game is played much like match play. However, rather than losing a point when you lose a hole, you instead lose a tee box. Start on the farthest tees (Champions tees) and play the hole. The person who loses the hole moves up to the next tee box for the next hole. This continues throughout the 9 or 18 holes you are going to play. The person at the farthest back tees wins.

GOOD FOR ALL OF US - One of the ways I like to add consequence is to do it with double benefits. My wife and I both work and we have two young children. For me to take a few hours to play or practice golf is a bit of a sacrifice for the whole family. However, if I set consequences that involve the family it helps me and it benefits my family. For example, if I shoot a certain (good) score the family gets to go out to dinner, or I get to give my wife a back massage. If I shoot a bad score, I do chores for the whole family. Both ways the family wins and I get to play golf, with consequences, and so I learn.

HAVE A GOAL – As we discussed in the goal setting chapter, before you play any round of golf you should have a goal, and then your consequences are weighted against that goal. (By the way, every once in a while throw in the goal to just have fun. It's unfortunate but the idea of fun is often overlooked in the game.)

For practice rounds you can add consequence the same way you do during range practice. Reward or punish the success of your goal. For tournaments it is a little different. If you are fixated on score, the reward and punishment will take care of itself. However, because golfers seek perfection they rarely dole out the reward as much as they should. It is not uncommon for a player to shoot a career score and the first thing they say is "If I only would have...". They are focused on what they could have done to improve a great score rather on what they did to create it. That is why I strongly suggest playing the "Good, Better, How" game after each round.

> ### *GOOD, BETTER, HOW*
> After each round you can play the Good, Better, How game. To play just start by talking about what was good about the round. Spend a lot of time here if you can. Then, describe what could be better and finally set up a plan that tells how to make it better. This way, the assessment of the round is more likely to be objective, accurate, and helpful rather than subjective, biased and hurtful. Remember, you are always teaching yourself something. You choose good or bad.

THE DOWN SIDE OF SUPERCHARGED LEARNING

So far we have talked about the up side of supercharged learning but there is a downside as well, and it can be quite powerful. Supercharged learning does not make judgment about what you are learning. Its job is to take in general information for a specific purpose. If something good happens supercharged learning will remember it and will encourage you to repeat that behavior. However, the more powerful side of supercharged learning is designed to keep you from harmful situations.

Remember the stripes in the tall grass? It could be a tiger or it could be a supermodel. Your first response is a fear response not a pleasure response because the reflexive memory is one of protection. Not only does this relate to golf, it relates to a very common occurrence in golf. This common occurrence is something you probably do, and I am sure you have seen professional golfers do it too.

- What happens when you hit a great drive? You take your eyes off of the ball and bend over to pick up the tee. You don't need to watch the ball because you know where it is going.

- What happens when you hit a bad drive? You watch the ball to see exactly where it will end up. You get upset about what happened and you probably kick yourself (metaphorically) several times before you even leave the tee box.

You may have caught on to the fact that the common occurrence with good and bad shots are exactly opposite of what they should be. By taking your eye off the ball and picking up your tee, you are breaking the positive cycle that was created by the great drive. Instead, you should watch the ball for the entire flight and then pat yourself on the back (metaphorically) several times before you even leave the tee box. I know you might be thinking that your playing partners will be wondering why you are watching the drive when you know where it will end up. Good. Let them. And don't worry about slowing the game down while you take a few seconds to admire your shot. Watching the ball land in the fairway will take much less time that looking for it in the woods.

Obviously you need to watch a bad drive to know where to look for your ball. However, immediately after you see the spot, break the cycle. Pick up the tee. Take just a moment and objectively assess what caused the problem and move on. Have a conversation with one of your playing partners or yourself (in your head please) about anything besides the shot. If you do this well you will have very little emotion associated with the shot in a matter of moments.

The point is that we do not emotionally charge an event unless we want to remember it. However, if you have committed an error in swing or decision you should remember what caused the error so you will not repeat it. Not long ago I hit a shot into a hazard just off the green. I knew that I couldn't ground the club in the hazard so I didn't take a practice swing. I hit a shot that went 10 feet past the hole and missed the putt. Rather than getting upset I took a moment to assess what had happened and decided that I should have taken practice swings outside of the hazard. Next time I am in a hazard I will remember the lesson learned from that hole. One goal we should all have on the course is to carry lessons with us, not baggage.

Carry lessons on the course, not baggage

Use supercharging to your advantage, not your disadvantage. The original system was designed for protection first and pleasure second. Human nature dictates you use it the same way. However, once again we see that to play great golf you often have to go against human nature. Switch it around during practice and on the course. Use the tools you have learned here to supercharge the things you want to learn and break the cycle on things you do not want to learn.

Supercharged learning is neither good nor bad. It is how it is used that makes it so

REVISITING THE ZONE

Early on in the book there was mention of the Zone. It would have been premature to belabor the point at that time because we had not yet established a foundation for the Zone. Remember, a building on a shaky foundation, now matter how well built, will still crumble under pressure. Again, from the Zone chapter comes the idea that the Zone requires two steps. Step 1: Create the skill necessary for success. Step 2: Get out of your own way and let the skill happen. If you fail to develop the basic skills, getting out of your own way won't help you much. Now that the foundation has been solidly constructed, it is time to revisit the Zone. Why is it that most people only occasionally visit the neighborhood of the Zone while others seem to have taken up residence on Zone Street?

Those individuals who rise to the occasion time after time have several things in common. Many books have tried to capture exactly what these common things are. However, one common omission in these books is the issues of relevance. Indeed, relevance has been a secret known by many a great player. Although the principle is based on the latest advances in cognitive neuroscience, these great players have practiced with relevance so that they can execute shots when it really matters. Take for example Ben Hogan's "miracle shot" at Merion in 1950 during the U.S. Open. In his book, Hogan described the 2-iron played to "a well-trapped, slightly plateaued green from about 200 yards out." Hogan commanded a master performance to force a play-off, and he delivered. He won the playoff the following day.

Entering the 2004 Masters Phil Michelson was labeled the "best player never to win a major." The back nine at Augusta National is no picnic but it is often the nine that determines the tournament's champion. Mickelson knew this as he sizzled the nine with 31. Still, he needed a birdie on the 18 to win his first major, to win the Masters. His approach shot was good but adrenaline drove it 18 feet past the pin, and above the hole. Don't be fooled by the television, the green has a wicked slope from back to front. Putting the ball off the green from where Mickelson stood was not unheard of. The crowd around the 18th green was remarkable. It was easily 10 people deep around the green and more than 100 yards down the fairway, and yet from the time Mickelson started to line up the putt it was silent. He knew he had to make it. There would be no turning back from this one. The putt rolled and the crowd buzzed. At the ball approached the hole the buzz turned into a roar and as the putt dropped the crowd exploded. Mickelson beat Ernie Els by one stroke to win the 2004 Masters Championship and for the next year and a half he lived on Zone Street.

Many players, like Jack Nicklaus, made clutch shots and putts so often that they seem almost routine. Remember, for example, in the 1972 U.S. Open at Pebble Beach Golf Links when Nicklaus needed a great shot on the par-3 17th hole? That day, as most, there was a stiff, gusty, ocean breeze which required Nicklaus to hit a 1-iron to a hole that seemed only a few paces from the ocean behind it. Nicklaus commanded yet another Zone performance, hitting the flagstick and ending up 6 inches from the cup. He went on to win the tournament.

Certainly Tiger Woods has had more than his share of Zone performances. One that comes to mind was on the 72nd hole of the

2000 Bell Canadian Open. Woods was in a fairway bunker with the tournament on the line. He hit a 6-iron over water to a pin tucked deep in the back right of the green. He went on to birdie the hole and win by one shot. With this win he became only the second man in history to hold the Canadian Open, British Open, and U.S. Open at the same time.

What is it that these people have? Like I said, volumes can and have been written about each but the real question is can we translate information about great performers into a form that can help you? The answer is clearly yes. You see, one thing that all of these people seem to have in common is relevance. They practice with it and they play with it. In other words, they have been there before. In fact, there have been there many times before, and I am not just talking about being there in a tournament.

I opened the book by giving an example of Ryan Moore's clutch performance at the Western Amateur and I'll complete this chapter with another of his Zone performances. When he entered the 2005 Bell Canadian Open Ryan had only been playing on tour for a few months. As he approached the tee shot on the 18th hole he was two shots down and needed a birdie and help from the leader, Mark Calcavecchia, to have a chance at his first PGA victory. As I saw it, this wasn't just an opportunity to win. It meant that Ryan would be the first player since Tiger to earn his tour card straight out of college and that meant not having to go through Q-School. This would be an incredible feat considering Ryan would only get seven tour exemptions to get his card (while most PGA members play more than 20 tournaments). The Canadian was the fifth of his seven tournaments and at this point he had only earned about $25,000 of the $635,000 he needed to get the card. This win would go a long way toward securing his card.

Stepping on the 18th tee box Ryan really needed a good drive to give himself a chance at birdie. Unfortunately, in three previous tournament rounds and a practice round he had not hit the fairway, so a good drive was easier said than done, especially under pressure. First time in four days he bisected the fairway with a perfect drive. He was 207 yards from the pin with a little wind in his face. Knowing he was a little pumped up, he chose a 5-iron and stuck it to within 2.5 feet of the hole and tapped in his birdie putt. He did what he had to do under pressure to give himself a chance to win. Unfortunately for Ryan, Calcavecchia didn't give him much, paring the last hole for a one shot victory. However, the second place finish earned Ryan $440,000 and more importantly allowed him additional tournaments to secure his card, which he did two tournaments later.

After the round I asked Ryan if he knew how important the last hole was to his quest for his card. He looked at me with some confusion and told that he didn't even think of his tour card, the moment and the win was all that mattered.

How do players like Ryan get to where they can hit the shots when it counts? They know how to get it done because they have been there before. They live their golf life embracing the consequences of each shot. If you ever get a chance to play with Ryan, try to give him a putt, no matter how long or short it is, he will not take it.

"They don't give you putts on tour" he will tell you.

The great ones know what science is now discovering I think it would be fitting to end this section with the best example of this that I can think of. In the January 2007 of GolfDigest (pg 99) Tiger Woods was asked about his practice. Tiger seeks knowledge as well if not better than anyone in the game, and yet it is his intuition and nature that hits home in the quote that epitomizes practice with consequence.

"As a kid, it's the way I learned to excel, to put myself in challenging positions. When I'm out practicing alone, I still do the same thing, like imagine some announcer going, *Here's Tiger Woods on the 18th hole, tied with Ben Hogan, Jack Nicklaus, and Bobby Jones. Can he put this 3-wood on the right side of the fairway?* It's always about that inner battle. Can I or can I not do it? You're heart's going. That's the beauty of it."   **– Tiger Woods**

Remember, every putt, every shot, in practice or in a tournament, counts for something if you let it. Use this to your advantage.

Summary and Reminder

In chapter X, I mentioned the saying *"If you give a man a fish he eats for a day. If you teach him to fish he eats for a lifetime."* I believe this with conviction, and so the idea behind the exercises along the way and the appendices at the back of the book is to teach you how to fish rather than just throwing you in and seeing if you catch something. Nevertheless, I do realize that there has been quite a bit of information presented in this book. This summary chapter is written to help remind you of key points. I think of this like watching a movie for a second (or third) time. The first time you see the movie you might remember the gist of it but may forget specifics. I'm sure at this point this is not surprising to you based on what you know about how we learn.

The summaries and reminder statements are presented in the order they appeared in the book in case you do want to look up the details. So you should be able to find them easily, but not too easily. You want some challenge after all.

SAYINGS AND SUMMARIES FROM PRACTICE TO LEARN, PLAY TO WIN

- ♦ Ability – Interference = Your Best Golf

- ♦ Great swings don't just happen, they are earned

- ♦ Decide that how you are playing now is not good enough. Decide you want more.

- ♦ Free your mind so you can free your weapon

- ♦ First you must develop the skill then free your mind

- ♦ A good mindset can't overcome bad skills. Hard work does not equal smart work, and smart work is what gets the job done

SUMMARY

As you well know, a good mindset can go a long way in getting a job done right. There will be times when you use the methods described in this book that it is difficult and without the right mindset it can be frustrating, so much so that you may want to go back to your old ways. Don't give in. Realize that to change means that something is different and one of the ramifications of this is that you may take a step back before you make a leap forward. If you have the right mindset you are more likely to be patient and buy into the process that will take you to the next level.

- ♦ All practice is not equal

- ♦ Proper practice can be a powerful ally or a frustrating foe. You choose.

- ♦ Habits of good must be replaced by habits of great

- ♦ You have to be willing to fall if you are going to learn to fly.

- ♦ You have to be willing to let go of good if you want to be great.

SUMMARY

Regardless how you define your good and your great golf, you can't be good and great at the same time. If you want to be better than you are now you need to do something different than you are doing now. In many cases this means letting go of the habits you have and replacing them with better habits, or at least those that are more consistent with your goals. This is yet one more time when mindset is important. Realize that to change means that you are rocking the boat and sometimes this means the boat tips a little. Know that when you take a step back, if you stay the course, your next move will be a leap forward.

- ♦ No challenge equals no learning

- ◆ Low challenge is one of the reasons that you can hit great shots on the practice range but not hit the same great shots on the course
- ◆ Good practice performance does not necessarily mean good learning
- ◆ Leave your ego home when you go to practice.
- ◆ Struggle on the range so you don't have to struggle on the course.
- ◆ "Repetition" does not always equal "Remembering"
- ◆ Practice doesn't make perfect. Practice makes permanent.

SUMMARY

People have been fooled for a long time into thinking that good practice performance means good learning, which in turn means good performance on the course. It's a natural assumption really. Why would you think any differently? Now you know that the brain works much like a muscle: you have to stress it for it to grow. In the weight room you wouldn't think twice about working to failure to get stronger. The same mindset should hold for learning the golf swing. I'm not talking about getting so tired you start hitting bad shots, I am talking about using your brain, stressing your brain, while you practice. The challenge, when appropriate, creates learning.

- ◆ You need an accurate and reliable source of information
- ◆ Learning is optimized when practice is appropriately challenging
- ◆ The challenge has to match the performer
- ◆ The better you are, the less feedback you should be given

SUMMARY

All the hard work in the world won't get you to where you want to go if it is hard work done in a misplaced manner. In other words, you have to know what you are doing and how to do it to get it done. There are a lot of moving parts to the golf swing and so we all need help from time to time. Get feedback from a teacher but only when you need it. Just like everything else, learning happens through struggle. The feedback can keep you moving in the right direction and then hard work will pay off. Finally, remember, the better you are the less often you should get feedback. Don't be fooled into thinking that more is better. It most certainly is not. Always match the feedback to the ability. More ability = less feedback.

- ◆ Number of balls hit ≠ amount of learning

- ◆ Focus on quality, not quantity

- ◆ Challenge yourself in practice so you feel less challenged in competition

- ◆ When you can stop fearing bad shots on the range you will take a major step to stopping the fear of bad shots on the course

- ◆ Good tempo can save a lot of bad swings

- ◆ Keep the club consistent if your swing is inconsistent and keep the clubs inconsistent if your swing is consistent

- ◆ Getting the answer right is not the key to learning. Learning how to solve the problem is the key to learning

SUMMARY

When you practice, focus on how well, not how much. Science and application have demonstrated that quality is much more important in leaning than quantity. Start practice with tempo drills, think about what you are doing and what you are working on in practice today as you are hitting balls, and then end with tempo drill. Be consistent and diligent in your practice regiment and always use the appropriate challenge.

- ◆ Discovery is like a treasure hunt. You are looking for the pot of gold known as great golf

- ◆ Make the puzzle as simple as possible rather than complicate it by adding layers

- ◆ Closing your eyes allows you to better focus on your positions and retrain your limbs for the proper position

- For you to learn how to do something you have to do something

- Write it down to remember it

- Make sure the process is sound before you focus on the results

- The more extraordinary your discipline in the early stages, the more extraordinary your progress

- The better the treasure map, the easier it is to rediscover where you buried the treasure

SUMMARY

There are three goals of practice; discovery, re-discovery, and refinement. By writing notes during your practice session you are helping all three goals. Keep in mind which goal of practice you are trying to accomplish today and set up your practice accordingly. For discovery, engage your forgetful memory. Experiment by hitting a lot of balls (no more than five in a row) and thinking about how ball position, grip, and swing impact the ball flight. With re-discovery, take a look at your notes from previous practice and the process will happen quickly. With refinement, quality rules. Hit fewer balls and think about each shot. Put yourself in scenarios like you are playing the course. Put some reward and punishment on the shots you hit. Make them count for something.

The difference between limiting and empowering beliefs is like the difference between trying not to lose and trying to win.

- Never underestimate the power of honest belief

- Goals present the destination, the process presents the means

- Be patient but tenacious when it comes to your goals

- Focus on the short term goals while keeping in mind the prize at the end

- Embrace the challenge and choose excellence

- Role models serve two purposes: they can provide advice

or guidance, and they can compress time

♦ Who are your role models? Who will help you feed the good dog?

♦ Go into each practice session with a purpose

♦ Choose 2-3 main goals. The rest will come along for the ride

SUMMARY

Goals are the roadmap to your success. They keep you on task and provide you with motivation. Remember to set up a goal, plan, and action (GPA) for practice and play and stick to it. In the long run it will serve you better than trying to hit a moving target. Look at your goals on a daily basis and have someone help you stay on track (goal keeper). Use role models in life and find out how they did what you want to do. Spend time making good goals and always go back to them to guide your decisions.

♦ See it and you are on your way. Feel it and it will be yours.

♦ Relevance causes permanence

♦ There is no doubt that people have a difficult time performing when the pressure is on. They practice with no consequences and play with lots of them. The system isn't set up to perform well under these circumstances.

♦ Get uncomfortable when it doesn't really matter and you will be more comfortable when it does

♦ Make practice count by adding consequence

♦ Challenge yourself in 'practice' see the rewards in competition

♦ Carry lessons on the course, not baggage

♦ Supercharged learning is neither good nor bad. It is how it is used that makes it so

♦ Every putt, every shot, counts for something if you let it. Use this to your advantage.

SUMMARY

Once you have developed a strong foundation of good practice habits and you are ready to supercharge your learning, do so with consequences. Place a wager with yourself on each round or each practice session. Challenge yourself when you play and don't give up on any shot or any hole. Don't give yourself putts. Create a situation where you learn from every shot and every putt, even if what you learn is how good it feels to do it right.

Appendix One: Glossary of Terms

AMYGDALA

The amygdalae (plural of amygdala) are primarily involved in the formation of memories associated with emotional events. The stronger the emotion (to some extent) the stronger the memory is stored.

CHALLENGE POINT

The point at which you are optimally challenged for learning. At this point you will struggle during practice but your learning will be optimized for the course.

CONSTANT PRACTICE

Constantly practicing the same thing. For example, on the practice range it is common to see a person hitting a 7-iron to the same target time after time.

DISCOVERY

The act of trying to discover something that will help you play better.

DRIVING RANGE PLAYER

The type of player that looks good on the driving range but cannot transfer that performance to the course.

DWELL TIME

Is the time that your club dwells (or stays) in address before you actually take the club back.

ELABORATION

The act of elaborating or attaching meaning. In golf, this can be by thinking of positions or feeling that you are trying to achieve during the swing.

EXPERIENTIAL FEEDBACK

Information you can get without the need for a coach or teacher. The ball flight, the click of a shot, and the feel of your body as you hit the ball are all considered experiential feedback (aka, proprioception.)

FEEDBACK

Information coming from an external source such as a teacher or video. Technically this type of feedback is known as knowledge of results.

GOAL KEEPER

Someone who will hold up the mirror for you, holds you accountable for your actions. They help keep you on track and encourage you.

HIT AND DRAG PUTTS

Hit and drag putts are those putts that immediately after you hit the putt you realize it will miss so even before it stops rolling you reach out with your putter and drag the ball back.

HIT AND SCRAPE

At the driving range, hit a ball, scrape another one from the pile right away, and hit that one. This is a method of repetitive practice. Bad repetitive practice.

INSTRUCTIONAL FEEDBACK

information fed back to a person by a teacher, coach, video camera. This type of feedback is called is instructional feedback because it is used to instruct the player.

MASSED PRACTICE

means that you practice en masse. In other words, you practice more than you rest.

PRIMITIVE BRAIN

This is the lower brain that evolved a long time ago for protection.

PROCESS (PERFORMANCE) GOALS

Goals are things like "I will focus on each shot." Performance goals are about the present.

PROPRIOCEPTION

Feedback coming from internal sources such as your muscles and joints. The feelings you have during a swing is an example of proprioception. Often times this is confused with the misnomer "muscle memory."

REDISCOVERY

Is when you had 'it' at some point, then you lost it, and now you are trying to find it again.

REFINEMENT

This is when you have already discovered what you want in your swing and you are tying to make that your habit.

REPETITION

Repeating the same thing over and over. In this book repetition is practicing the same shot time after time rather than varying a shot. Technically this is known as rote repetition and does little for enhanced learning.

RESULT (OUTCOME) GOALS

Are "I will win the tournament." Outcome goals are about the future

ROLE MODEL

Is a person who serves as your council, either literally or figuratively. The literal role model is a person you go to with questions of "What would you do?"

SHORT-TERM GOALS

Are set for the short time, a day, a week, a month. They allow you to see immediate improvements in performance

SPACED PRACTICE

Means that you rest more than you practice. It is similar to constant practice in that you are often repeating the same shot with the same club with very little time between shots. Generally this is the opposite of what you do on the course.

TASK DIFFICULTY

Task difficulty is defined simply: The difficulty of the task based on accuracy, coordination, and environment, which in this case refers to the circumstances surrounding the task.

TOURNAMENT PLAYER

The type of player that creates appropriate challenge during practice so that they can excel when the pressure is on, like in a tournament.

VARIABLE PRACTICE

The type of practice in which you change, or vary, the club and/or target frequently during practice. Variable practice is the opposite of constant practice and is generally considered a better way to practice.

Appendix Two: References

BOOKS USED AND RECOMMENDED

Collins, J. (2001). *Good to Great.*

> Harper Collins publishing, Inc., New York, NY

Gallwey, W.T. (1988). *The Inner Game of Golf.*

> Random House of Canada Limited, Toronto.

Jerome, J. (1980). *The Sweet Spot in Time.*

> Summit books, New York, NY

Wiren, G., Coop, R., & Sheehan, L. (1985). *The New Golf Mind.*

> Simon & Schuster, Inc., New York, NY

Johnson, S. (2004). *Mind Wide Open.*

> Simon & Schuster, Inc., New York, NY

Kriegel R., & Kriegel, M.H., (1984). *The C-Zone.*

> Random House of Canada Limited, Toronto.

Parent, J. (2002). *Zen Golf.*

> Random House New York, NY

RESEARCH ARTICLES

Guadagnoli, M.A., & Lee, T. (2004).
Challenge Point: Framework for Conceptualizing the Effects of Various Practice Conditions in Motor Learning.
> Journal of Motor Behavior, 39(2), 212-224.

Guadagnoli, M.A., Davis, M., & Holcomb, W.R. (2002).
The Efficacy of Video Feedback for Learning the Golf Swing.
> Journal of Sport Science.
> Also reprinted in the text, Science of Golf IV.

Guadagnoli, M.A., McDaniels, A., Bullard, J., Tandy, R.D., & Holcomb, W.R. (2001).
The Influence of Video and Verbal Information on Learning the Golf Swing.
> In P.R. Thomas (Ed.), Optimising Performance in Golf, 94-103.
> Brisbane, Australia: Australian Academic Press.

Guadagnoli, M.A. & Kohl, R.M. (2001).
Utilization of Knowledge of Results for Motor Learning.
> Journal of Motor Behavior, 33(2), 217-224.

Guadagnoli, M.A., Weber, S. T., & Holcomb, W.R. (1999).
The Relationship Between Contextual Interference Effects and Performer Experience on the Learning of a Putting Task.
> Journal of Human Movement Studies, 37:19-36.

Guadagnoli, M.A. & Holcomb, W.R. (1998).
The Effects of Variable and Constant Practice on the Skill of Putting.
> Science of Golf III, Martin Farally & Alastair Cochran (Eds.). Human Kinetics, Champaign, IL.

Guadagnoli, M. A., Dornier, L. A., & Tandy, R. (1996).
Optimal Length of Summary Knowledge of Results: The Influence of Task-Related Experience and Complexity.
> Research Quarterly for Exercise and Sport, 67, 239-248.

Kohl, R.M. & Guadagnoli, M.A. (1996).
The Scheduling of Knowledge of Results.
Journal of Motor Behavior, 28(1), 233-240.

Appendix Three: Sample Practices

EXAMPLE: 2-HANDICAPPER

Date: **June 25, 2007**

Consequence

Goal: **I will be a great speed putter. From 30-feet away I will leave at least 80% of my putts within three feet of the hole.**

Goal Keeper: **none for the session, practice by myself**

Role Model: **Dwaine Knight**

Plan: **This practice will be a 35 minute session starting at 12:00 pm**

- **12:00-12:05 Tempo putts to an area 30-35 feet away**

- **12:05-12:15 3-5 footers, aim at specific sides of the hole and play with pace on the putts**

- **12:15-12:25 hit putts for distance, alternate uphill and downhill putts each time, go through routine, hit putts 20-35 feet**

- **12:25-12:30 10 puts to a hole 30 feet away. Go through routine each time, must make 8 of 10 or I lose a beer each miss.**

- **12:30-12:35 Tempo putts to an area**

Assessment

Before and after level of expertise rating: Before __5__ After __7__

(0 to 10 with 10 being Tiger Woods)

Level of commitment (10 being outstanding)
8 – this was good but I will do better here next time

Good, Better, How

What was good?:
I maintained my focus well. Hitting tempo putts before I started putts to the hole really helped. I did a great job reading the break.

What will I do better?:
I can still do a better job maintaining focus. I can get the radius of my 30-foot putts tighter. I made 7/10. Most of the putts were short. I can be more aggressive.

How will I do it?:
I will use more variable practice before I test myself that way I will think before every putt. I will even change from downhill to uphill putts every 2-3 putts. I will make sure every putt up to 20 feet is past the hole.

EXAMPLE 19-HANDICAPPER

Date: **June 25, 2007**

Consequence

Goal: **From 20-feet away I will be able to hit 6/10 putts no more than three feet from the hole.**

Plan: **This practice will be a 35 minute session starting at 12:00 pm**

- ◆ **12:00-12:05 Tempo putts to an area**

- ◆ **12:05-12:15 2-4 footers, 3 putts from the same distance and line before I move to the next putt, remember to take a few seconds between putts and don't rush it**

- ◆ **12:15-12:25 hit putts for distance, practice uphill for five putts and then downhill for five putts. hit putts 15-25 feet**

- ◆ 12:25-12:30 10 puts to a hole 20 feet away. Go through routine each time, hit five putts in a row from above the hole and five putts in a row from below the hole. I must make 6 of 10 within a 3 foot circle or I lose a beer each miss.

- ◆ 12:30-12:35 Tempo putts to an area

Assessment

Before and after level of expertise rating: Before __5__ After __7__

(0 to 10 with 10 being Tiger Woods)

Rate your level of commitment (10 being outstanding)
8 - this was good but I will do better here next time

Good, Better, How

What did I do well?:
I maintained my focus well. Hitting tempo putts before I started putts to the hole really helped. I did a great job reading the break.

What will I do better?:
I can still do a better job maintaining focus. I can get the radius of my 30-foot putts tighter. I made 7/10. Most of the putts were short. I can be more aggressive.

How will I do it?:
I will use more variable practice before I test myself that way I will think before every putt. I will even change from down hill to uphill putts every 2-3 putts. I will make sure every putt up to 20 feet is past the hole.

PRACTICE WORKSHEET

Date:

Goal:

Goal Keeper: Role Model:

Plan:

Assessment

Before and after level of expertise rating: Before ____ After ____
(O to 10 with 10 being Tiger Woods)

Level of commitment (10 being outstanding):

Good, better, how

What was good?

What will I do better?

How will I do it?

Appendix Four: Example Goal Sheets

GOAL:

Over the next three months I will improve my average putts per round by two putts.

What is my leverage?

I am a very good ball striker and my putting is holding me back. If I want to be a great player I must be a great putter. I will be a happier person and have more fun playing if I am putting well.

Goal keeper: **Dwaine Knight**   Role model: **Ryan Moore**

Short term goal 1: **By the end of this month I will increase my ability to lag putt so that I will get 9 of 10 balls within a 3-foot circle from 15 feet away.**

Short term goal 2: **By the end of the following month I will be able to make 7 of 10 putts from 6-feet.**

PLAN:
- ♦ I will get one putting lesson at the beginning of each month.
- ♦ Each day for one month I will spend 10 minutes practicing pace putts. For each putt I hit I will go through my routine and focus just like in a match. Once a week I will challenge someone to a pace putt competition.

- Each day for the following month I will spend 10 minutes practicing 3- 5 foot putts and 5-7 foot putts. On each of these putts I will go through my routine and focus just like in a match. Once a week I will challenge someone to a 5-7 foot putting competition.

ACTION ASSESSMENT:

I did a great job sticking to my plan. I reminded myself of my goal and my plan each day before I practiced. I practiced every day even if it was in my living room. My putting average improved three strokes per round and now I am ready for a new goal. I think I am a good putter now but my next goal will be to make me a great putter.

GOAL SHEET

GOAL:

What is my leverage?

Goal keeper: Role model:

Short term goal 1:

Short term goal 2:

PLAN:

ACTION ASSESSMENT:

Printed in the United States
89055LV00001B/59/A